T0323805

APHASIA
THE BASICS

This book provides a comprehensive yet accessible introduction to aphasia, or loss of language, a complex condition that affects approximately a third of stroke survivors.

It describes the varied manifestations of aphasia on speech, comprehension, reading, and writing. Chapters explore how aphasia presents across different languages and in bilingualism, as well as the impacts of aphasia on a person's life and the effects for family members. The text also considers recovery in aphasia and how that recovery can be enhanced by a range of interventions. All topics are informed by extensive research and personal accounts of individuals living with aphasia.

Anyone interested in language needs to know about aphasia and will find here the perfect beginner's guide. The book provides an invaluable introduction to aphasia for students of speech and language therapy, health professionals and others with an interest in stroke care. It also offers easy-to-read answers to many of the questions posed by family members of stroke survivors.

Jane Marshall is an honorary professor at City, University of London, UK. She worked clinically as a speech and language therapist before specialising in aphasia research. Resulting in well over 100 publications, her research has explored numerous aspects of aphasia, including sentence processing in aphasia, jargon aphasia, aphasia in Deaf users of sign language, and therapy for people with aphasia.

THE BASICS SERIES

The Basics is a highly successful series of accessible guidebooks which provide an overview of the fundamental principles of a subject area in a jargon-free and undaunting format.

Intended for students approaching a subject for the first time, the books both introduce the essentials of a subject and provide an ideal springboard for further study. With over 50 titles spanning subjects from artificial intelligence (AI) to women's studies, *The Basics* are an ideal starting point for students seeking to understand a subject area.

Each text comes with recommendations for further study and gradually introduces the complexities and nuances within a subject.

ISLAMIC PSYCHOLOGY
G. HUSSEIN RASSOOL

IMITATION
NAOMI VAN BERGEN, ALLARD R. FEDDES, LIESBETH MANN AND BERTJAN DOOSJE

SELF AND IDENTITY
MEGAN E. BIRNEY

PSYCHOPATHY
SANDIE TAYLOR AND LANCE WORKMAN

EVOLUTIONARY PSYCHOLOGY
WILL READER AND LANCE WORKMAN

WORK PSYCHOLOGY
LAURA DEAN AND FRAN COUSANS

FORENSIC PSYCHOLOGY (3RD EDITION)
SANDIE TAYLOR

APHASIA
JANE MARSHALL

For more information about this series, please visit: www.routledge.com/Routledge-The-Basics-Series/book-series/B

APHASIA
THE BASICS

Jane Marshall

Routledge
Taylor & Francis Group

LONDON AND NEW YORK

Designed cover image: The cover image was created by a group of people with aphasia who took part in the INCA project (inclusive digital content for people with aphasia) at City, University of London.

First published 2024
by Routledge
4 Park Square, Milton Park, Abingdon, Oxon OX14 4RN

and by Routledge
605 Third Avenue, New York, NY 10158

Routledge is an imprint of the Taylor & Francis Group, an informa business

© 2024 Jane Marshall

The right of Jane Marshall to be identified as author of this work has been asserted in accordance with sections 77 and 78 of the Copyright, Designs and Patents Act 1988.

All rights reserved. No part of this book may be reprinted or reproduced or utilised in any form or by any electronic, mechanical, or other means, now known or hereafter invented, including photocopying and recording, or in any information storage or retrieval system, without permission in writing from the publishers.

Trademark notice: Product or corporate names may be trademarks or registered trademarks, and are used only for identification and explanation without intent to infringe.

British Library Cataloguing-in-Publication Data
A catalogue record for this book is available from the British Library

Library of Congress Cataloging-in-Publication Data
Names: Marshall, Jane, 1958- author.
Title: Aphasia : the basics / Jane Marshall.
Description: Abingdon, Oxon ; New York, NY : Routledge, 2024. | Includes bibliographical references and index. |
Identifiers: LCCN 2023055783 (print) | LCCN 2023055784 (ebook) |
ISBN 9781032466675 (hardback) | ISBN 9781032466644 (paperback) |
ISBN 9781003382737 (ebook)
Subjects: LCSH: Aphasia.
Classification: LCC RC425 .M2995 2024 (print) | LCC RC425 (ebook) |
DDC 616.85/52--dc23/eng/20240221
LC record available at https://lccn.loc.gov/2023055783
LC ebook record available at https://lccn.loc.gov/2023055784

ISBN: 978-1-032-46667-5 (hbk)
ISBN: 978-1-032-46664-4 (pbk)
ISBN: 978-1-003-38273-7 (ebk)

DOI: 10.4324/9781003382737

Typeset in Bembo
by MPS Limited, Dehradun

CONTENTS

FIGURES

ACKNOWLEDGEMENTS

I am hugely indebted to the many people who have taught me about aphasia and supported my career as a clinician and researcher. First of all, to the many stroke survivors with whom I have worked clinically and who have taken part in our research: thank you for your generosity in sharing your time, efforts, and insights. Thank you to members of the speech and language therapy team at Queen Mary's Hospital, Sidcup, who provided me with an inspirational student placement and first clinical post, particularly Jan Dorling, Carol Sacchett, Caroline Rucker, Sally McVicker, and Betty Semery; I also want to remember the inestimable Liz Clark who is alas no longer with us. Thank you to my wonderful PhD supervisors and fellow researchers: Shula Chiat and Tim Pring. Thanks also to Shula for feeding back on an early section of the book. Thank you to current and past members of the amazing Aphasia Team at City, University of London: Nick Behn, Anna Caute, Naomi Cocks, Madeline Cruice, Niamh Devane, Lucy Dipper, Julie Hickin, Katerina Hilari, Rachel Holland, Jayne Lindsay, Sally McVicker, Katie Monnelly, Rebecca Moss, Morganie Naidoo, Sarah Northcott, Abi Roper, Richard Talbot, Kate Swinburn and Celia Woolf. Thank you to our lovely colleagues from City's Centre for Human Computer Interaction Design, particularly Stephanie Wilson, Julia Galliers, Tracey Booth, and Timothy Neate. Thank you to Bencie Woll and Jo Atkinson for the opportunity to explore sign language aphasia and for making this such an enjoyable experience. Thank you to the funding bodies who have supported our aphasia research: The Stroke Association, The Tavistock Trust for Aphasia, the MRC, the EPSRC, The Barts

Charity, Garfield Weston Foundation, Bupa Foundation, and Sir Halley Stewart Trust. Thank you to Sarah Scott for letting me use your story and feeding back on the relevant section. Thank you to Abi Roper, Cat Andrew, and Niamh Devane for all your help with the images. Thank you to Olivia Elliot for the advice about Kiswahili. Thank you to Tori Sharpe and Ceri McLardy from Routledge. And finally thank you to Jerry for everything else.

INTRODUCTION

Masie was in her 50s and working as a civil servant when she had a stroke. Regaining consciousness in hospital she was faced with life changing losses. She was paralysed down the right side of her body and unable to talk. Over time Masie learnt to walk again and recovered some halting and fragmented speech. Here is a brief example of her in conversation, several years after her stroke:

> Jane: What did you do over the weekend?
>
> Masie: Mother's Day ... er Nicola (daughter's name) ... meals ... flowers ... er chocolates

We can tell a lot from this sample. Masie was not confused. She remembered her weekend and was able to convey some of what had happened on the Sunday, when she had celebrated Mother's Day. She also understood the question. However, her response was limited to a few words, separated by long pauses and unconnected by sentence structure. The lack of verbs in this sample is striking, indeed her speech was overwhelmingly composed from isolated nouns. This sample has no obvious errors; the words she did use were correct. However, there were many other instances when this was not the case. For example, on another occasion she tried to retell the story of Cinderella. She was unable to think of the word "slipper", saying "boot" instead. Masie was acutely aware of her speech difficulties. She expressed frustration over her word finding problems and reacted to her errors by shaking her head and saying "no". Masie's problems affected her language, not simply speech

DOI: 10.4324/9781003382737-1

pronunciation. Nevertheless, she struggled to articulate some words particularly when they were long.

Like Masie, Rachel also had a stroke, in her case when she was 75 and retired from an academic career in art history. Rachel, too, acquired a right sided paralysis and a severe language impairment. But there the similarities end. Even from the early days post stroke, Rachel's speech was fluent and effortlessly articulated. However, it was almost impossible to understand, being composed from streams of non-words (utterances like "gudermini" and "switickus"). Pauses in Rachel's speech were rare, and, unlike Masie, she did not express frustration over her difficulties with communication. Rather, Rachel seemed surprised and occasionally indignant when other people failed to understand her. Aspects of Rachel's speech were intact, most notably the intonation line. Indeed, if heard from a distance or against background noise her speech sounded deceptively unimpaired. The retained rhythms in Rachel's speech enabled her to communicate aspects of meaning. Her feelings were often clear from her tone of voice; and it was usually possible to judge whether she was asking a question, making a statement, commiserating with someone, or refuting a point. A wicked humour also came through. For example, she was able to mimic other people's accents, albeit in meaningless non-words. In conversation, it was difficult to judge whether Rachel understood what others said, as her replies were rarely interpretable. But, like Masie she showed no signs of confusion. For example, she recognised her friends and knew when they were due to visit. She lived in a care home and was beset with problems over her laundry. Yet she always knew if she has been given the wrong clothes. She retained her interests in art, visiting galleries, and looking at art books.

Masie and Rachael both had strokes affecting the left hemisphere of the brain. We know this because they each had a **Computerised Tomography** (CT) scan, which is a form of X-ray that can reveal areas of organ damage. You will recall that they both had paralysis to the right side of the body (also called a right **hemiplegia**). This was a further clue. Motor control is contralateral, i.e., the left hemisphere of the brain is responsible for controlling the right side of the body and vice versa. Therefore, the fact that Masie and Rachel had right sided paralysis pointed to left hemisphere strokes.

In most people, the left hemisphere is the dominant hemisphere of the brain and the neural centre for language. As a result, damage here often leads to **aphasia** or loss of language. This was true for both Masie and Rachel. Yet, as we have seen their cases were strikingly different, not only in terms of their speech symptoms but also in their seeming awareness of those symptoms. An obvious question is why did these differences arise? Numerous other questions could be asked. Was their understanding of speech intact, and how did we know? Was their reading and writing affected and, if so, were the problems similar to those seen in speech? What was the impact of aphasia on their lives and on the lives of their friends and family members? Masie and Rachel both spoke English. How does aphasia manifest in other languages or in bilingual language use? Perhaps most importantly, did Masie and Rachel experience any language recovery, either spontaneously or in response to rehabilitation? This book will attempt to answer these questions, not just in relation to Masie and Rachel but with respect to aphasia in general. I also hope to show why the study of aphasia matters. This is partly so that we can better understand and, hopefully, help with the dilemmas faced by the many people who acquire aphasia every year. But also because aphasia offers a unique and fascinating window onto the nature of language. Indeed, before we go any further into aphasia, I need to introduce a few linguistic concepts.

INTRODUCTION TO LANGUAGE

At the risk of stating the blindingly obvious, all spoken languages contain words. These comprise at least two elements: meaning and form. The meaning, or **semantics**, might be imagined as a cluster of features that define the word; so "cow" is an animal, with four legs and a tail, found on a farm, that gives us milk, etc. The form, in the case of spoken words, is the **phonology** or sound structure. "Cow" is made up from two speech sounds or two **phonemes**: the consonant "c", pronounced /k/ and the vowel "ow" pronounced /aʊ/. Substituting one of these sounds will result in another word ("now", "key") or in a non-word ("fow"). Phonology concerns the way sounds are used in a language and is principled. Only a limited inventory of speech sounds feature in any language, and which sounds are included varies across languages. So, as an English speaker, I will only use click sounds non linguistically, perhaps to imitate a horse's hooves or express disapproval. Whereas a speaker of

Xhosa will use the same sounds as part of the phonological make up of words. Another principle concerns how sounds can be combined within words. English words, for example, can start with clusters of two or three consonants as in "sting" and "string", but not with clusters of four: "sctring". There are also constraints over which sounds can combine. "Mbwa", for example, is an illegal form in English but not in Kiswahili (where it means dog).

Words group into classes. So, we can divide words into verbs (denoting events, actions, and states), nouns (denoting the entities involved in those events), adjectives (denoting the properties of nouns) and adverbs (denoting how verbs are enacted). Nouns, verbs, adjectives, and adverbs are sometimes referred to as **content words**, because they express much of the meaning in a sentence. They also make up the overarching category of **open class words**, so called because we are always adding to their number. For example, new nouns are created to describe new inventions ("cryptocurrency") and new verbs to label previously unheard-of activities ("chillaxing"). Open class words contrast with **closed class words**. These are words that perform a primarily grammatical function, such as pronouns ("he", "they"), determiners ("the"), connectives ("and", "yet", "but"), and auxiliary verbs ("he *was* walking"). They are a closed class in that new additions are not made to the set.

It is astonishing to reflect on how easily healthy language users deploy their vocabulary. The average American English speaker is thought to know over 40,000 words (Brysbaert et al., 2016), yet can summon those words in the blink of an eye. Of course, we all occasionally make errors with words. But these errors are rare and systematic. So, if we substitute one word for another the error is likely to be either semantically or phonologically related to the target. We may call a pencil a "pen" but are very unlikely to call it a "car". Our errors also obey the phonological constraints of our language. An English speaker is highly unlikely to import non-English sounds into speech errors, or combine sounds illegally. As we shall see, for people with aphasia effortless word retrieval is often lost. Rather, recovery of words is a struggle and errors may proliferate. However, we shall also see that even in aphasia the principles underpinning lexical processing are still observed. We shall also see that aphasic errors often reflect word classes, with some types of words affected more than others.

There is more to language than just words. Languages also have grammatical structure or **syntax**. This is the means by which a language combines words and phrases to express relational meanings. In English, a key syntactic device is word order. In the following sentences we know who is doing what to whom through the order of the words, and reversing that order reverses the meaning:

Rishi ridiculed Keir.

Keir ridiculed Rishi.

However, word order is not the only device. Take the following sentence:

Rishi was ridiculed by Keir.

Here the word order is deceptive. If we just pay attention to the order of nouns around the verb, we might come away with the impression that Rishi was doing the ridiculing. In fact, the auxiliary verb (was), the verb inflection (-ed) and the preposition (by) marks this as a passive sentence in which the word order has been flipped. This passive sentence illustrates the role of closed class words, together with word **inflections**, in the construction of syntax. These elements are essential for many other structures, such as questions:

Why did Keir ridicule Rishi?

Negatives:

Keir did not ridicule Rishi.

And sentences with embedded clauses:

Rishi, who hoped to win the argument, ridiculed Keir.

They also convey many other aspects of language, such as tense:

Boris walks the dog.

Boris walked the dog.

And plurality:

> A shoe.
>
> Shoes.

My examples are drawn from English, but of course syntactic markers feature in all languages. Indeed, many languages have more elaborated syntactic markers than English, for example including grammatical gender. Given its complexity, it is unsurprising that syntax is often a casualty of aphasia. However, we shall also see that syntactic skills can be preserved in aphasia, either wholly or in part.

A further property of language is that it has different modalities. So, a competent language user must not only produce spoken language, but also comprehend the speech of others. Most (but not all languages) also have written modalities, i.e., reading and writing. Of course, these modalities are acquired later than speech, typically through formal instruction, and we cannot assume that everyone who has had a stroke was previously literate. When exploring aphasia, it is essential to consider all the language modalities, especially as they often dissociate. Thus, one person may have good production of speech, but poor speech comprehension, while another may reverse this pattern. We also see dissociations between speech and writing, e.g., where writing is more or less preserved than speech. We need to understand these patterns in order to know what language resources are and are not available to the individual.

To understand aphasia, we also need to appreciate the distinction between language and communication. Language is a formal system first learnt through exposure to the language of the child's community and elaborated through educational instruction. It is our primary method of communication. However, we use many communicative devices alongside and in addition to language. As a minimum, these include gesture, facial expression, and intonation or tone of voice; but, depending on context, they can extend to mime, drawing, emojis, smoke signals, flags, you name it. We shall see that, in aphasia, a surprising amount of communication may be achieved despite the loss of language. Indeed, Rachel has already illustrated how aspects of meaning may be communicated purely through intonation. We shall also see that recovery of communication is a primary focus of rehabilitation; and while this may involve direct work on language skills many other options are available.

I began this section by saying that all spoken languages contain words. But speech is not the only medium for language. There are also hundreds of sign languages used by Deaf people across the world. These are mutually incomprehensible languages that have evolved and are transmitted within Deaf cultural groups. So, American Sign Language is quite distinct from British Sign Language and different again from the many sign languages used in Asian and African countries. Sign languages are governed by the linguistic principles described above. For example, signs, like spoken words, have phonological structure. This is composed not from sounds, but from manual features, such as handshape. Signs also combine into syntactically structured sentences that express relational meanings. And we shall see that sign languages, like any other language, are susceptible to aphasia.

Having thought about some of the properties of language I now want to introduce the basic architecture of the brain and some neurological terms that will be employed in this text.

THE BRAIN AND LANGUAGE

The brain comprises two cerebral hemispheres (left and right) a cerebellum and brain stem. The hemispheres are divided into four lobes: frontal, parietal, temporal and occipital (see Figure 1.1). Different areas of the brain undertake distinct functions. For example, the occipital lobe is crucial for vision; the parietal lobe is important for processing sensory information; and many aspects of cognition, such as planning and behaviour regulation, are controlled by the frontal lobes. In most people, language processing is conducted mainly in the dominant, left hemisphere of the brain. There are key regions for language processing in the frontal and temporal lobes. These are called **Broca's** and **Wernicke's areas** after 19th-century scientists who first identified them (see Figure 1.1 and Box 1.1). However, language is not confined to these areas. Rather, it is thought to depend on a distributed neural network across much of the left hemisphere. Areas of the right hemisphere are also active during language and communication tasks, indicating some bilateral control of language.

Brain function is maintained by a complex system of arterial blood supply. Interruption to this supply will cause a stroke. Such

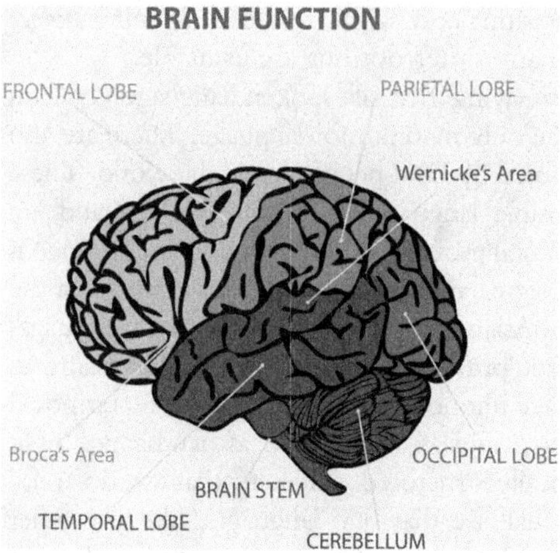

BRAIN FUNCTION

Figure 1.1 A drawn image of the left hemisphere of the brain showing the frontal, parietal, temporal and occipital lobes, and Broca's and Wernicke's areas.

interruption may occur because a blood clot blocks an artery, or because of a fissure in the arterial wall, causing a bleed. When the blood supply is cut off, the region of brain at and beyond the point of failure is starved of oxygen, with resulting damage. Stroke effects, therefore, vary, depending on the location of arterial failure.

When stroke, and other neurological impairments were first investigated, the nature and location of the damage could only be established via autopsy, i.e., the removal and examination of the brain after death. It is now possible to image sites of neurological damage in the living brain, either via computerised tomography (CT), which uses X-ray technology, or via **Magnetic Resonance Imaging** (MRI), which uses a combination of strong magnetic fields and radio waves. Both techniques produce 3D brain images delineating lost or impaired tissue. As a result, we can now relate clinical signs to patterns of neural pathology, which, in the context of aphasia, has significantly advanced our understanding of which areas of the brain are responsible for language. A third imaging technique is **functional MRI**. This evaluates blood flow in the brain, so shows which areas of the brain are most active while a person carries out a given task. It has been a further powerful tool in demonstrating the neurological basis of language.

Box 1.1 Paul Broca and Carl Wernicke

Although there are accounts of aphasia in classical and medieval texts, systematic study of the condition began in the 19th century, particularly in France. Much of this study centred on the localisation debate. On one side of the debate, the localisationists argued that cognitive functions were conducted by specific brain regions, which, in the case of language, were thought to be in the frontal lobe. On the other side, the holists argued that functions were distributed throughout the brain, without specialised areas.

Paul Broca, French physician, anatomist, and anthropologist, produced definitive evidence in favour of the localisationists. Broca was working in the Bicetre Hospital where he had the opportunity to examine a patient called Leborgne. Then in his 50s, Leborgne had suffered from epilepsy since his youth and had progressive loss of speech, that began in his 30s. He had also subsequently acquired a right sided paralysis of the arm and leg. Although Leborgne's comprehension of language was said to be intact, he had no speech beyond the repetitive utterance of "tan". Leborgne died of an infection soon after the examination, enabling Broca to conduct a brain autopsy. This revealed a large frontal, left hemisphere lesion, in the region now known as Broca's area (see Figure 1.1). Broca concluded that the frontal region was the seat of articulated language, although he was yet to declare hemispheric specialisation. Broca went on to examine further cases of what he called "aphemia" (loss of expressive language), all of whom had left hemisphere frontal lesions. In 1865, this led Broca to pronounce that we speak with the left hemisphere of the brain.

In 1874, the German physician Carl Wernicke published "The Symptom Complex of Aphasia". This work described a different type of aphasia, featuring fluent, but disordered speech, impaired speech comprehension and disrupted reading. In contrast to Broca's cases, such instances of "sensory aphasia" arose from lesions in the posterior part of the left hemisphere, now known as Wernicke's area (see Figure 1.1). Wernicke combined his data with Broca's to propose a model of the neural basis of language. This model included a motor centre for speech production (Broca's area) and an acoustic centre for comprehension (Wernicke's area) and hypothesised neural pathways between them. Wernicke argued that lesions to different parts of this model caused the varying presentations of aphasia.

The brain regions identified by Broca and Wernicke are still recognised as crucial to the processing of language. However, advances in brain imaging have revealed that language is served by a more complex neural network than they originally supposed, including structures beneath the cortex (surface). Broca preserved Leborgne's brain in alcohol, making it available to posterity. As a result, a number of research teams have been able to scan it, using both CT and MRI technology. These scans have revealed widespread damage in the left hemisphere, extending deep into the brain and into both the parietal and temporal lobes (Dronkers et al., 2007). Thus, even in Leborgne's case, damage beyond Broca's area was contributing to his severe aphasic symptoms.

REHABILITATION

The disabilities caused by stroke rarely resolve spontaneously. Therefore, rehabilitation is needed. This aims to recover lost skills and enable the person to carry out everyday activities despite their impairments. Managing the emotional and social consequences of stroke may also be a target. Ideally, stroke survivors will have access to a multi-disciplinary team of rehabilitation specialists. As a minimum this should include physio, occupational and speech and language therapists. Physio therapists support rehabilitation of movement and advise on movement aids. Occupational therapists particularly focus on activities of daily living, such as washing, dressing, and cooking. They also advise on aids and adaptations to the home. Rehabilitation of aphasia is led by speech and language therapists (also termed "speech pathologists" in other English-speaking countries). They are responsible for assessing a person's language and communication skills, and delivering therapies aiming to restore communication. Speech and language therapists often advise family members and friends about aphasia and suggest strategies for improving communication in the home. Much of the aphasia research cited in this book was conducted by speech and language therapists. Their work will also be focussed in Chapter 7 which deals with the rehabilitation of aphasia. I should reveal, here, that I qualified and practised as a speech and language therapist.

SUMMARY AND TAKE-HOME MESSAGES

In this chapter we met two stroke survivors: Masie and Rachel. Their marked, but differing language symptoms introduced aphasia and opened up some of the conundrums of the condition. The chapter familiarised the reader with linguistic concepts that will feature in the upcoming text and provided a brief introduction to the anatomy of the brain and to methods of brain investigation. I introduced the professionals involved in stroke rehabilitation, and particularly the role of speech and language therapists. Hopefully this chapter has readied you for a more detailed exploration into the nature of aphasia.

Finally, some notes about the text:

- Masie and Rachel are pseudonyms. They have both been reported in journal articles using the initials MM for Masie and RMM for Rachel. Many other people with aphasia will be described in this book, usually drawn from examples in the literature. When referring to these individuals I will use the identifiers from the original paper, which may be pseudonyms or initials. Occasionally, I refer to individuals who have appeared under their real name, for example in online videos.
- As you saw in the section about language, this book occasionally uses phonemic transcription. This is a method of reporting speech sounds. It is used because alphabetic script does not necessarily indicate how a word is pronounced. To illustrate, think about the different pronunciations of "c" in "cow" and "ceiling", or the vowels in "bow" (archery) vs "bow" (when meeting the king). The use of phonemic transcription is indicated by forward slashes (/ /) framing the relevant symbols. So, the transcription for cow is /kaʊ/ and for ceiling is /ˈsilɪŋ/.
- "Deaf" is capitalised in this book to denote membership of a linguistic and cultural group, in the same way that we capitalise "English". When "deaf" is used without capitalisation it refers to audiological, rather than cultural status. As someone in my mid-60s, I am becoming increasingly deaf. I have not, however, switched language or cultural allegiance, so have not become Deaf.
- Many points in this book are supported by references to the literature. The citations in the text indicate the author(s) and date of publication, such as (Lundgren & Brownell, 2016). When there are more than two authors the phrase "et al." is used after the first author, which simply means "and everyone else". The full reference is provided in the reference list at the

end of each chapter. I occasionally highlight references that you may want to follow up.

- You will have noticed that some of the more unfamiliar terms used in this text are in **bold**. These are explained when they are introduced but are also defined in the glossary at the end of the book.

REFERENCES

Brysbaert, M., Stevens, M., Mandera, P., & Keuleers, E. (2016). How many words do we know? Practical estimates of vocabulary size dependent on word definition, the degree of language input and the participant's age. *Frontiers in Psychology*, 7. https://www.frontiersin.org/articles/10.3389/fpsyg.2016.01116

Dronkers, N. F., Plaisant, O., Iba-Zizen, M. T., & Cabanis, E. A. (2007). Paul Broca's historic cases: High resolution MR imaging of the brains of Leborgne and Lelong. *Brain*, *130*(5): 1432–1441. doi:10.1093/brain/awm042. ISSN 0006-8950. PMID 17405763

2

WHAT IS APHASIA?

Aphasia is a language impairment arising from brain damage, usually in the form of a stroke. It is common. Every year, about 100,000 people have a stroke in the UK (https://www.stroke.org.uk/what-is-stroke/stroke-statistics) and roughly a quarter of the survivors acquire a persisting aphasia (Ali et al., 2015). It is estimated that 350,000 people are living with aphasia in the UK (https://www.stroke.org.uk/what-is-aphasia).

Aphasia is almost always the result of left hemisphere damage, given that this hemisphere plays the major role in language processing. However, there are rare exceptions to this rule, when aphasia occurs after a right hemisphere stroke or brain injury. This is most likely in left handers, where brain dominance may be less lateralised. When it occurs in right handers it is called **crossed aphasia**.

A striking feature of aphasia is its variability, in that no two people with aphasia are quite alike. There are, however, broad types of aphasia, which I will introduce in this chapter. Two of these types are exemplified by Masie and Rachel. These are Broca's aphasia and Wernicke's aphasia.

BROCA'S AND WERNICKE'S APHASIA

Broca's aphasia, exemplified by Masie, is named after Paul Broca, the 19th-century French physician and anthropologist who we met in Box 1.1. A form of non-fluent aphasia, this condition is characterised by hesitant, fragmented speech. There are frequent pauses while the speaker searches for words or struggles to convey their ideas. Broca's aphasia is also marked by **agrammatism**, or an absence of grammar.

DOI: 10.4324/9781003382737-2

You will remember that Masie's speech lacked any sentence structure. Words were not linked together. There were no verbs and no closed class words. There were also virtually no grammatical inflections, although the perceptive reader will have spotted that she did use plural markers, e.g., in the word "chocolate**s**". As a result of these omissions, we often have to guess what Masie is trying to say. It seems likely that the chocolates mentioned in her speech were a gift from her daughter, but without sentence structure it is difficult for Masie to make this clear. These characteristics of Masie's speech are typical of agrammatism. To summarise, people with this form of aphasia consistently show: reduced sentence structure and word order, omissions of grammatical markers (closed class words and inflections), and better production of nouns than verbs. Any syntactic elements that are retained are also most likely to be attached to nouns. So, inflections may be realised on nouns, e.g., to mark a plural, but not on verbs. Thus, an agrammatic speaker may say "walk" rather than "walks" or "walked". Having said that, there are variations in severity. So, speakers with mild agrammatism may produce truncated sentences, such as: "man drinking" and "girl eating ice cream". However, they will struggle to convey complex forms like passives, questions, or sentences with an embedded clause.

Broca's aphasia is often accompanied by a problem with speech pronunciation called **dyspraxia** or **apraxia**. This is a difficulty in sequencing the movements required for speech production. It is often marked by oral groping behaviours, as the person struggles to move their tongue and lips in order to pronounce the word that they are trying to say. Unsurprisingly, long words and words with complex sound sequences are particularly problematic for people with dyspraxia. So "car" may be said successfully, while "Maserati" is not. Dyspraxia is not due to paralysis in the oral muscles, i.e., the tongue and lips are still functioning normally. As a result, people with speech dyspraxia have no problem eating and drinking. Automatic speech is also relatively intact. So, a person with dyspraxia who burns their finger may let out a perfectly articulated swear word. Their problem is with the conscious planning of speech production. As a mark of this, errors are inconsistent. So, when trying to say the word "sister" the person may say "sitter" on one occasion and "sisser" on another.

Wernicke's aphasia, exemplified by Rachel, is also named after a 19th-century scientist (see Box 1.1). Speech in this form of aphasia is fluent but extremely difficult to understand. For this reason, it is often referred to as **jargon**. As we saw with Rachel, jargon may be composed entirely from non-words, or **neologisms** (newly coined words). In other speakers, there is some recognisable language, but with much of the open class vocabulary replaced with non-words. Here is an example:

> I can show you then what is a zapricks for the elencom the elencom with the pidland thing.
>
> [KC describing a picture of a telephone; Butterworth, 1979]

The non-word errors produced by people with Wernicke's aphasia are really puzzling. If you or I make a speech error, we are much more likely to produce a real word than a non-word. So where do these errors come from in cases of aphasia? Research has taught us some interesting things about aphasic neologisms (Marshall, 2006). First of all, neologisms are typically made up from the phonemes (speech sounds) within the speaker's language. For example, the neologisms produced by English speakers with aphasia very rarely contain non-English sounds such as clicks. Neologisms obey other phonological constraints. So, when listening to an English speaker of jargon you are very unlikely to hear a neologism such as "spkritch", with an opening cluster of four consonants.

Robson and colleagues (2003) analysed a large number of neologisms produced by a speaker with Wernicke's aphasia. They counted the number of times that each phoneme occurred across all the recorded neologisms. There were interesting discrepancies. For example, there were 88 instances of the sound /s/ (the first sound in the word "sing") in the speaker's neologisms, compared to just seven instances of the sound /ʒ/ (the final sound in the word "beige"). The researchers then ranked all the sounds from the most to the least common. Intriguingly, the resulting order was very similar to the ranking of sounds in the host language (in this case English). So, sounds that are common in neologisms, like /s/, are also very common in English; whereas sounds that rarely occur in neologisms, like /ʒ/, are also infrequent in English.

What does this all mean? It seems that neologisms are not totally arbitrary. Rather they are produced with at least some reference to the speaker's language. There is more evidence to back this up. In some research, it was possible to compare neologisms to the speaker's intended target word. The methods take a bit of explaining here, so some readers may just want to take this on trust. For those who are feeling strong, further details are summarised in Box 2.1.

Box 2.1   Comparing neologisms to target words (Pilkington et al., 2019)

Emma Pilkington and her colleagues studied the neologisms produced by ten speakers with Wernicke's aphasia.

Each person was asked to read aloud and (on a separate occasion) repeat 64 words. In a third task they were asked to name the items shown in 64 pictures. In each task, the responses were recorded and transcribed; i.e., the exact sounds used in every response were noted down. All of the participants in this research made frequent errors on these tasks, including many neologisms.

The researchers were interested in whether the neologisms produced by these speakers at all resembled the target words. For each neologism, they counted the number of sounds that were shared between that neologism and the target. They multiplied this number by two, then divided the result by the total number of sounds in both the target and the neologism (this method took account of the length of the response in the calculation). The resulting figure, which they called the Phonological Overlap Index (POI), was a score for the resemblance between the target word and the neologism.

An obvious concern is whether some resemblance occurred by chance. For example, a speaker might say "nitel" for the target "train". This neologism has two sounds from the target ("t" and "n") and would score .44 using the above POI formula. But did these shared sounds occur just by chance? To address this, the researchers did a cunning thing. They took each speaker's neologisms, together with their target words, and shuffled them. As a result, the neologisms were now paired with a random word. The researchers calculated the POI of these random re-assignments, and compared the result with the genuine pairings. They found that the scores for the true pairings were significantly higher than the chance pairings. With just one exception this was true for all speakers on all tasks. The researchers concluded that there was a genuine resemblance between the neologisms and the intended target words, at a rate that exceeded chance. These speakers clearly retained some knowledge of the words in their language and were tapping into that knowledge when generating neologisms.

This research showed that, for the studied speakers, there was a resemblance between the neologism and the target. In other words, some of the sounds in the target word were present in the neologisms, and at rates that exceeded chance. Again, it seems that neologisms are not purely arbitrary. Rather they are the result of failed attempts to access real words, albeit attempts that have been severely derailed by the person's aphasia.

While neologisms are common in Wernicke's aphasia, some speakers produce jargon that is composed mainly from real words. Unfortunately, this form of jargon is still very difficult to understand, mainly because the selection of words is highly anomalous, as illustrated in the following example:

> *Hangs around the place ... got two horses and a tail and the mouth changes from various aspects of the bird.*
> [RG describing a picture of a dog; Marshall et al., 1996]

It is difficult to uncover the intended meaning from this sample. Yet, the content is not totally unrelated to the picture. Features of the dog are mentioned ("mouth" and "tail") and other animal terms are used ("horses" and "bird"). Again, the jargon is not random, but seems to be the result of failed word selection. We might hypothesise that this speaker has not fully summoned the semantic specification of the words he wants to use. As a result, he uses terms that are related to the target, but still wide of the mark. In line with this interpretation, this form of speech is often described as **semantic jargon**.

We have established that Wernicke's aphasia is characterised by highly disordered speech. Yet, as was described with Rachel, these speakers rarely attempt to correct or supress their errors. Indeed some, like Rachel, seem surprised and even angry when they are not understood. There are also accounts of people with Wernicke's aphasia who refuse rehabilitation for their speech. These signs suggest that people with Wernicke's aphasia may not be aware that they have a language difficulty.

Lack of awareness of neurological deficit is a recognised phenomenon and is termed **anosognosia**. In stroke, it usually occurs following right hemisphere damage. For example, there are accounts of survivors of right hemisphere strokes who deny that they have a paralysis, despite being dependant on a wheelchair. It seems that, at least some individuals with Wernicke's aphasia have anosognosia. Yet assessing this is difficult. For example, if we ask the person about how they perceive their problems, we will probably not understand their response. With Rachel we were dependent on observation, and here the results were curious. Rachel's aphasia did not simply affect her speech. Her writing was also impaired, indeed she struggled to write even single words. Yet, Rachel clearly knew when her writing attempts were wrong, for example she shook her head and crossed out her errors. We concluded that Rachel's anosognosia was selective, and confined to the monitoring of speech.

Some experimental studies have further investigated self-monitoring in Wernicke's aphasia. The participants in this research were asked to make judgements about the accuracy of their speech. For example, in one study they had to name a pictured object and then point to a tick or cross to signal whether their response was correct or not (Sampson & Faroqi-Shah, 2011). These individuals often produced neologisms and other errors in place of the pictured name, but then judged their response to be correct. It seemed that it was difficult for these individuals to monitor their speech.

Why does self-monitoring break down in Wernicke's aphasia? In many cases there is an impairment of speech comprehension; i.e., the speech of others is misunderstood. This points to a general problem with listening to and interpreting speech, which may explain why self-monitoring fails. Indeed, Purcell and colleagues (2019) found that the ability to monitor errors was related to comprehension scores in five people with jargon speech. However, researchers have argued that other factors may also play a role in reducing awareness. Way back in 1981, Weinstein proposed that there may be an element of psychological denial, as the person struggles to retain a sense of their former self, before the impact of stroke. It has also been suggested that there may be a problem of attention. In other words, people with Wernicke's aphasia may be unable to carry out the dual task of speaking and listening to their own speech (Marshall et al., 1998).

So far, I have described two forms of aphasia in which the symptoms are almost diametrically opposed. Broca's aphasia is marked by meaningful, but non-fluent speech, frequent articulation difficulties, and good self-awareness. Most people with

Broca's aphasia also show relatively preserved understanding of speech, although this may not extend to the understanding of complex sentences. While, in Wernicke's aphasia speech is fluent and easily articulated, but, in severe cases, virtually stripped of meaning. Here, recognition of the difficulties may also be lacking and, allied to this, comprehension of other people's speech is often impaired.

There is a further contrast. Some readers may have spotted that the samples of speech in Wernicke's aphasia quoted above retain grammatical features. For example, here the neologism is housed within an intact syntactic phrase:

I can show you then what is a zapricks

So, while syntax is impaired in Broca's aphasia it may be relatively intact in cases of Wernicke's aphasia. Allied to this is a dissociation between the word classes. People with Broca's aphasia omit many closed classed words (such as "a" and "then"), while these are often retained in Wernicke's aphasia. Conversely, at least some open class words, particularly nouns, are achieved in Broca's aphasia, while these are often absent or erroneous in Wernicke's aphasia. These contrasts suggest that language processing entails distinct operations that may be impaired or spared in aphasia. We can hypothesise that one operation deals with syntax, and associated closed class words, while another deals with the recovery of content words. It seems that for people with Broca's aphasia, syntactic operations are severely impaired, while content word processing is relatively retained; whereas in Wernicke's aphasia the pattern reverses.

The contrastive skills and weaknesses in Broca's and Wernicke's aphasia reflect differing areas of neurological damage. Broca's aphasia typically arises from damage to part of the left frontal lobe, including, but rarely confined to, Broca's Area (see Figure 1.1). While in Wernicke's aphasia the damage is normally further back in the brain, affecting the left temporal lobe (see Wernicke's area imaged in Figure 1.1). The precise roles of these brain regions in language processing are debated; but most agree that the frontal region plays a role in speech production and possibly grammar, while the temporal region is engaged in speech comprehension and the processing of word meaning.

ANOMIC APHASIA

Not all cases of aphasia can be categorised as Broca's or Wernicke's. A further broad type is **anomic aphasia**. **Anomia** means loss of words, so the key symptom of anomic aphasia is the inability to produce the names of things, people, and places. As with all forms of aphasia, people with anomic aphasia vary in severity. Those who are severely affected may struggle to produce any open class vocabulary. When anomia is less severe, some words are still accessed while others are not. Here the patterns are interesting. For example, words that are frequently used in the speaker's language are more likely to be retained than words that are infrequent. So, if asked to list animals, a person with anomic aphasia may be able to name common animals like "cat" and "dog" but not the less common ones, like "lion" and "elk". Abstract words, such as "democracy" and "idea", are also typically more difficult than concrete words, like "castle" and "train". Age of acquisition is another determinant, with early acquired words being more resistant to anomia than words that are acquired later. Of course, these factors interact. The word "dog" is common in English, concrete and usually acquired early in childhood; while the word "serendipity" is low frequency, abstract and, if known at all, probably acquired in school or even adult life. "Serendipity" is, thus, very unlikely to be produced by a speaker with anomia.

Why do these patterns matter? First of all, they help us to predict words that might be problematic for people with anomia. They also suggest some strategies for improving communication. For example, many people with anomia learn to substitute difficult words with more common alternatives ("car" instead of "vehicle"). The patterns are also informative about how words may be organised in our brain. It seems that how often we use a word affects its relative availability, making common words more readily available than uncommon ones. Indeed, the factors that typically predict whether or not words can be accessed in anomia are also seen to affect how quickly unimpaired speakers produce words. So, you and I may still name rare animals, such as "aardvark" and "iguana", but we will do so more slowly than the common-or-garden "cat" and "dog".

What happens when a speaker with anomia is stuck for a word? They may grind to a halt or engage in a lengthy word search.

Expressions of frustration are common ("oh, what's it called?"), demonstrating awareness of the difficulty. Some speakers can describe features of a blocked word, for example saying "in the bedroom" for wardrobe. These responses are known as **circumlocutions**. On other occasions the word may be substituted by an error. Errors are often related to the target. So, some speakers make **semantic errors**, for example replacing a target word with an item from the same category ("table" instead of "chair"). Other errors are phonologically related, for example saying "char" instead of "chair".

The varying responses in anomia are not random but reflect how words are normally processed in the brain. As described in the Introduction, words have both semantic and phonological properties, and these must be recovered for the word to be produced. If both semantic and phonological processing fails, nothing will be forthcoming. Other instances reflect a more selective breakdown. If semantic information is retrieved, but not phonology, the person may be able to convey some of that information via a circumlocution. Partial retrieval of semantic information may result in a semantic error. On other occasions, the meaning of the word may be accessed together with some (but not all) information about its phonology. In these instances, a **phonological error** is probable.

There is another interesting characteristic of anomia, in that people with this form of aphasia can often be cued. For example, a person with anomia might be unable to name a picture of an elephant. But if they are provided with the first sounds of the word ("el"), they might succeed. The fact that a word can be cued suggests that it is not permanently lost. It is as if the word is still available in the person's brain, but just out of reach. Giving the person a nudge, in the form of a cue, enables them to grab hold of it. Related to this, are the potential implications for therapy. If a word can be cued once, repeated cuing in therapy may make that word permanently more accessible. We will return to this in Chapter 7.

Anomic aphasia can arise from damage to different areas of the left hemisphere. In some individuals the stoke has affected posterior parts of the brain, while others have more frontal damage. This suggests that producing words involves a neural network that is distributed over several brain regions and damage to any part of that network can derail production.

CONDUCTION APHASIA

A fourth category of aphasia is **conduction aphasia**. People with this form of aphasia have fluent, grammatical speech. But there are word finding difficulties and frequent phonological errors. These speakers show awareness of their errors and often try to correct them. This may result in strings of phonological errors related to a target, such as "baselaw, lacelaw, basecall, casecall ..." for baseball (example from Buchsbaum, et al., 2011), a characteristic that has been termed **conduite d'approche**. A further marker of conduction aphasia is poor repetition and poor performance on short-term verbal memory tasks. So, people with this form of aphasia find it difficult to retain and repeat back words and phrases. In contrast, understanding of words is good (see Bartha & Benke, 2003 for an overview of the symptoms of conduction aphasia).

It is argued that conduction aphasia reflects an impairment in processing word phonology. This causes the phonological errors and repetition problems. It is as if these speakers cannot hold onto the sounds of words in their heads. In line with this, production is affected by phonological complexity, i.e., naming and repetition of long, polysyllabic words is particularly impaired (Goodglass, 1992).

Conduction aphasia was thought to arise from damage to the neural fibres that connect Broca's and Wernicke's area in the brain, a structure called the **arcuate fasciculus**. It was thus known as a disconnection syndrome, in which communication between the speech production and speech comprehension areas is severed. More recent evidence has challenged this view. This has shown that damage leading to conduction aphasia typically occurs in an area around the posterior part of the **sylvian fissure**, at the junction between the parietal and temporal lobes. Functional MRI studies with healthy language users have shown that this area of the brain is involved in short-term verbal memory tasks, e.g., where the person being tested has to rehearse and repeat back a string of spoken words (Buchsbaum et al., 2011). Thus, damage to this area is consistent with the symptoms of conduction aphasia.

GLOBAL APHASIA

The final type of aphasia that I want to introduce is **global aphasia**. Here all aspects of language are impaired. So, people with global aphasia have limited speech, poor comprehension of speech, and impaired reading and writing. Speech may be virtually eliminated, or reduced to a few stock phrases, such as "I can't". Some individuals have one repetitive utterance that emerges every time they attempt to speak. Repetitive utterances are often, but not always, expletives (swear words), possibly because such words are produced more automatically than other items of vocabulary. In line with this, some people with global aphasia can recite learnt sequences, such as days of the week or months of the year. Global aphasia is usually the consequence of widespread damage to the left hemisphere of the brain.

CLASSIFICATIONS OF APHASIA: SOME CAVEATS

I have described five broad types of aphasia: Broca's aphasia, Wernicke's aphasia, anomic aphasia, conduction aphasia, and global aphasia. I now want to unsettle the reader by underscoring the individual variation seen in this condition. This variation operates within as well as between the categories. So, two people may share the diagnosis of Broca's aphasia, but display marked differences, for example in the extent and nature of their agrammatism. We have already seen that types of jargon in Wernicke's aphasia vary, particularly with respect to the production of non-word errors. Forthcoming chapters will show that comprehension of language also varies across individuals, regardless of the speech presentation, as does reading and writing. There is the further complication that the boundaries between aphasia types are not clear cut. In other words, symptoms that are typical of one category of aphasia may also be seen in others. A good example here is word finding difficulties. These are not simply observed in anomic aphasia; rather a problem with word retrieval is almost universal in aphasia. Finally, communication skills are not necessarily determined by classification. For example, an individual with global aphasia may achieve surprising communication success through the strategic use of pictures, gesture, and drawing.

For these reasons, many people argue against the classification of aphasia. If categorical diagnoses are used, they should be seen as broad descriptive terms. Full understanding of a person's aphasia requires individual assessment. As a minimum, we need to explore the extent to which language can be produced and understood, both in spoken and written forms, the ability to communicate despite the language impairment and the impact of aphasia on the person's life.

APHASIA AND COGNITION

Despite their severe aphasia we saw that neither Masie nor Rachel was confused. Masie lived in her own home, where she cooked basic meals, shopped, and took public transport to her therapy sessions. She used her limited language to describe events in her life, express opinions, and convey her interests. Although Rachel lived in a residential home, she was independent in many aspects of self-care, such as dressing. She recognised the staff and reacted with surprise when a new carer appeared. She remembered appointments and, with help from her friends, kept a simple diary. She navigated round the home without difficulty and knew the way to the local park. In all these respects Rachel was strikingly different from the many residents with dementia living in her home.

Masie and Rachel illustrate how aphasia is a disorder of language, rather than cognition. Providing there is no additional neurological impairment, people with aphasia can remember past and upcoming events. They can carry out daily living tasks and are oriented in time and place. Past interests will be retained, particularly if they are non-language dependent, as we saw with Rachel's continuing fascination with art.

Research has uncovered further cognitive skills in aphasia (Varley, 2014). For example, in one study people with agrammatic aphasia successfully carried out mathematical calculations (Varley et al., 2005). Other studies have shown that individuals with aphasia can make inferences about the beliefs of other people, a skill that is known as Theory of Mind. Apperly and colleagues (2006) demonstrated this with PH, a person with severe aphasia. He was shown videos in which one of the protagonists had a false belief. Here is an example. The film showed a man and a woman in a room with two boxes. The man places a green object in one of the boxes while the woman watches. The woman then leaves the room and while she is out of view the man moves the object from one box to the other. The woman then re-enters the room. At this point the video was paused and PH was asked to indicate where the woman would look for the green object. She, of course, had not seen the object being moved, so would have the false belief that it was in the original box. PH's responses on this task showed that he could make this inference, and consistently so. He was shown 12 false belief trials (intermixed with other types) making an error on just one.

Once again, it is now time to unsettle the reader. Although cognitive strengths have been demonstrated in aphasia, many studies paint a less rosy picture. These have shown that people with aphasia do less well on tests of cognition than comparative groups (Murray & Mayer, 2017). Areas of difficulty include attention, memory, and problem solving. To illustrate, Baldo and colleagues (2015) administered non-verbal intelligence tests to stroke survivors with and without aphasia. The aphasic group scored worst, particularly when the task involved high levels of reasoning. For example, they were impaired on a task in which they had to rearrange pictures to tell a story. Performance correlated with the degree of language deficit. Those with the most severe aphasia, affecting both comprehension and production, were poorest on the cognitive tasks.

It seems that research has uncovered cognitive strengths and impairments in aphasia. Why have these contradictory findings emerged? First of all, testing cognition in people with aphasia is difficult, particularly when the aphasia is severe. This is because most cognitive tests involve a degree of language, if only to understand the test instructions. Of course, researchers are sensitive to this problem. For example, they employ tests that are mainly non-verbal and explain them through demonstration. Nevertheless, language abilities may affect results. A further difficulty is knowing whether poor performance on a cognitive test is due to the aphasia, or some other factor. Strokes typically cause multiple problems, some of which relate to thinking and reasoning. Poor performance on a cognitive test could be due to these other stroke related difficulties, rather than the aphasia. Again, researchers are aware of this confound, which is why Baldo and colleagues used stroke survivors without aphasia as the comparative group.

Let's draw the findings together. People with aphasia do not have a global cognitive impairment, so are very different from people with most types of dementia. Despite this, many perform poorly on tests that involve problem solving and reasoning. Some of their difficulties may be due to testing factors, such as poor understanding of the task instructions, or to other stroke related deficits. However, these factors may not account for all the data. A further interpretation is that aspects of cognition require language. Baldo and colleagues argue that difficult cognitive tasks are supported by inner speech. In effect we talk ourselves through the problem. People with severe aphasia may be unable to generate this inner dialogue, with negative consequences for their reasoning skills. So, here is another instance where patterns in aphasia offer novel insights, in this case into the relationship between language and thought. Aspects of cognition can clearly progress without language, so can withstand aphasia. However, language may also scaffold thinking. So, when difficult cognitive tasks have to be performed people with aphasia pay a price.

NON STROKE APHASIAS AND PRIMARY PROGRESSIVE APHASIA

Although aphasia is caused most commonly by stroke, other forms of brain damage can give rise to the condition. For example, aphasia can result from tumours in the left hemisphere, or from surgery to remove tumours (Davie et al., 2009). Aphasia has also been observed in cases of traumatic head injury, for example as a result of a fall (e.g. Nishio et al., 2004).

In 1982, Mesulam described six individuals who had aphasia without having had a stroke. In all cases the aphasia was progressive. For example, word finding difficulties became worse over time, or were gradually accompanied by additional problems affecting comprehension. Crucially, in all cases, the problems were almost entirely confined to language. The affected individuals continued to live independently, hold down jobs, drive, maintain social and family roles. Some were given cognitive tests on which they performed well. Thus, global dementia was ruled out.

The condition described by Mesulam is now known as **Primary Progressive Aphasia** (PPA). It is caused by progressive degeneration of the brain regions that underpin language, particularly in the frontal or temporal lobes. For this reason, it is also referred to as Frontotemporal Lobar Degeneration (FTLD) or frontotemporal dementia. The degeneration is circumscribed, at least in the early stages of the disease, which explains why other cognitive functions are retained.

There are three types of PPA, depending on which brain region is most implicated (Gorno-Tempini et al., 2011). Bilateral damage to the temporal lobes is associated with Semantic Variant PPA (SV-PPA) also known as Semantic Dementia. Here there is a gradual loss of conceptual knowledge, affecting the meaning of words and objects. Although speech is grammatical and fluent, there are severe word finding problems. If asked to name pictures the person is likely to fail or make a semantic error (e.g., calling a horse a "dog" or "animal"). Object recognition is also poor, i.e., the person may respond to a picture by saying "I don't know what that is". Naming in semantic variant PPA typically cannot be cued (Jefferies & Lambon-Ralph, 2006). So, giving the first sound of a word does not help the person produce it. You will remember that this contrasts with post stroke anomic aphasia, where cues often trigger word production. It suggests that word knowledge is lost in semantic variant PPA, rather than simply out of reach. Over time, speech in SV-PPA becomes increasingly empty or devoid of open class vocabulary. Word comprehension also breaks down. The ability to repeat words and phrases is typically maintained, although often performed without understanding.

The second type of PPA is Progressive Non fluent Aphasia (PNFA), which is associated with damage to the left frontal lobes. Here the patterns are similar to Broca's aphasia. Speech is hesitant and agrammatic (lacking syntax). There are word finding difficulties, although the person continues to display object recognition. Repetition is poor. Single words are understood, although grammatically complex sentences are not. Speech pronunciation is often disrupted by apraxia. As the disease progresses the person may become mute.

The final type of PPA is Logopenic Variant (LV-PPA). It was described most recently, to account for individuals who did not fit the other two variants (e.g., Mahendra, 2012). Here speech is slow with frequent pauses and word finding problems. Unlike PNFA there is no agrammatism and no apraxia. Unlike SV-PPA naming errors tend to be phonological rather than semantic and there is retained object recognition. Repetition of words and phrases is poor. Logopenic variant PPA is associated with focal degeneration in the frontal lobes. However, the pathology is not entirely clear, and it is thought that some individuals may have early onset Alzheimer's Disease (Mahendra, 2012).

Primary progressive aphasia is rare. In 2011, Knopman and Roberts estimated that between 20,000 and 30,000 people were living with condition in the USA. This compares to an annual USA incidence of 200,000 for stroke related aphasia. You are, thus, much more likely to meet someone with aphasia due to a stroke than PPA.

While there are similarities between PPA and stroke aphasias, for example in some of the language symptoms, there are also important differences, most notably in the disease progression. In aphasia caused by stroke we can predict at least some improvement. This may occur spontaneously, particularly in the early period after the stroke, or as a result of rehabilitation (see Chapter 7). In contrast, PPA worsens over time, and in many cases there is eventual progression to cognitive domains beyond language. Treatments have been attempted in PPA, for example aiming to maintain language skills or enhance communication strategies. However, effects are typically constrained (Marshall et al., 2018).

This book will focus on stroke related aphasias. Reading suggestions are given below for those who wish to find out more about PPA.

Marshall, C. R., Hardy, C. J. D., Volkmer, A., Russell, L. L., Bond, R. L., Fletcher, P. D., Clark, C. N., Mummery, C. J., Schott, J. M., Rossor, M. N., Fox, N. C., Crutch, S. J., Rohrer, J. D., & Warren, J. D. (2018). Primary progressive aphasia: a clinical approach. *Journal of Neurology*, *265*(6), 1474–1490. https://doi.org/10.1007/s00415-018-8762-6

Kertesz, A., & Harciarek, M. (2014). Primary progressive aphasia. *Scandinavian Journal of Psychology*, *55*(3), 191–201. https://doi.org/10.1111/sjop.12105

RIGHT HEMISPHERE DAMAGE AND COMMUNICATION

So far, I have emphasised the role of the left hemisphere in language and stressed that aphasia almost always follows left hemisphere damage. Some readers may be wondering what happens when a person has right hemisphere damage (RHD) for example following a stroke, and particularly whether there are any consequences for communication.

As already stated, aphasia following RHD is rare. So, people who have had a right hemisphere stroke typically retain grammatically correct language, do not display word finding problems and can demonstrate understanding of both words and sentences. However, communication may not escape unscathed. Relatives may remark that their family member seems different. They may not engage so much in conversation, may lose the thread when telling a story, or fail to get a joke. Their speech may sound flat and less expressive than it did before the stroke.

Research involving people with RHD has identified subtle communication impairments, consistent with these observations. This has shown that discourse following RHD may go off topic or lack cohesion (Sherratt & Bryan, 2012). Difficulties with **prosody** (speech rhythms and intonation) have also emerged. Wright and colleagues (2018) asked four individuals with RHD to listen to recorded sentences and use the prosody to infer the emotion of the speaker. For example, one sentence was spoken in an angry tone of voice, so had to be matched with the word "angry" (rather than "sad", "disgusted", "fearful", "surprised", or "happy"). Three of the people tested found this difficult. In a separate task, all four individuals were unable to modulate their own speech to convey a given emotion. Figurative language can be a further site of difficulty. For example, a person with RHD may match an idiom ("he had a heavy heart") with a picture showing the literal rather than metaphoric meaning (Lundgren & Brownell, 2016). Cheang and Pell (2006) explored appreciation of humour. They found that some (but not all) people with RHD were unable to pick an appropriate punchline for a given joke.

These findings suggest that the right hemisphere does play a role in language, particularly in the processing of inferred aspects of meaning. And imaging studies, involving healthy language users, back this up. In one study, participants were asked to read and make judgements about the coherence of passages of text (Kuperberg et al., 2006). While they did this, their patterns of brain activation were tracked using functional MRI. In some of the texts, coherence was obvious. In others, it had to be inferred (see examples in Table 2.1 below). The researchers were interested in which parts of the brain became most active when inference was required. They found that the inference texts excited an extensive bilateral neural network, including specific areas in the right hemisphere.

Table 2.1 Examples of Stimuli used by Kuperberg et al., 2006

Text	Category
• The boys were having an argument. • They began hitting each other. • The next day they had bruises.	Highly related (coherence obvious)
• The boys were having argument. • They became more and more angry. • The next day they had bruises.	Intermediately related (inference required)

How does the right hemisphere contribute to language processing? One hypothesis argues that it has "coarse coding" semantic skills that complement those of the left hemisphere (Beeman, 2005). According to this proposal, the left hemisphere is good at recovering specific semantic information from words, and supressing irrelevant information. So, when hearing the sentence "he hurt his foot" the left hemisphere differentiates "foot" from other body parts and inhibits irrelevant interpretations, in this case arising from homophones (12 inches; a poetic foot). In contrast, the right hemisphere accesses diffuse semantic networks, including meanings that are unrelated to the given context. So, with the above sentence, words associated with foot, such as "hand", "leg" and "shoe", are activated as are the homophonic meanings. Such diffuse semantic information is useful for forming connections between words, or processing shades of meaning. It is particularly important for appreciating meanings that are implied but not stated, as is the case with inference, figurative expressions, and many aspects of humour.

The fact that the right hemisphere has language resources should be good news for people with aphasia. First of all, they may be able to exploit the subtle processing skills of their intact hemisphere. However, revealing these skills is difficult. Tasks involving idioms, humour or inference make heavy demands on all aspects of language, so will be beyond many people with aphasia. We can use observation, and this often suggests that people with aphasia *do* retain many of the subtle communication competencies that are threatened by RHD. We can observe people with aphasia using humour and picking up unstated meanings. Those with poor language comprehension often use context to infer what is being said, for example guessing that someone is asking for the salt at the dinner table. We have already seen how Rachel used prosody in her speech to convey aspects of meaning. She was also sensitive to the prosody of others, for example detecting irritation or impatience.

The language skills of the right hemisphere may also support recovery. In other words, they might enable the right hemisphere to take on language tasks that were previously accomplished by the left hemisphere. There is evidence that this can happen early in life. For example, Vargha-Khadem and colleagues (1997) report on a nine-year-old boy who acquired speech after surgical removal of his left hemisphere. The role of the right hemisphere in adult recovery is less clear cut, although cases have been reported in which regained language functions are associated with increased right hemisphere activation (Blank et al., 2003). We will return to this topic in Chapter 7.

To summarise, people with right hemisphere strokes rarely acquire aphasia. Many, however, have subtle problems with communication, particularly affecting implied and non-literal uses of language. This evidence, together with imaging studies involving healthy language users, indicates that the right hemisphere does play a role in language. One theory states that it helps to process word meaning, by accessing diffuse semantic networks. People with aphasia may still have recourse to right hemisphere semantic skills, and may engage right hemisphere processing within their recovery.

SUMMARY AND TAKE-HOME MESSAGES

This chapter introduced five types of aphasia: Broca's aphasia, Wernicke's aphasia, anomic aphasia, conduction aphasia, and global aphasia. It emphasised the variation seen in aphasia, even within these broad types.

It discussed how symptoms of aphasia are not arbitrary but reflect how language is processed in the brain. It emphasised that aphasia often reflects a partial rather than total breakdown in language function. As a result, some skills may be lost while others are retained. Even when errors are made, those errors may reveal residual language abilities.

Cognition in aphasia was discussed. It was emphasised that aphasia, unlike dementia, is not a cognitive impairment. Despite this, people with aphasia may perform poorly on some cognitive tests, possibly because they cannot generate the "inner speech" that helps us to solve difficult cognitive problems.

Non stroke aphasias were introduced and impairments following right hemisphere damage. The latter point to language skills in the right hemisphere which may still be accessed by people with aphasia.

REFERENCES

Ali, M., Lyden, P., & Brady, M. (2015). Aphasia and dysarthria in acute stroke: Recovery and functional outcome. *International Journal of Stroke*, *10*, 400–406.

Apperly, I., Samson, D., Carroll, N., Hussain, S., & Humphreys, G. (2006). Intact first- and second-order false belief reasoning in a patient with severely impaired grammar. *Social Neuroscience*, *1*(3–4), 334–348. 10.1080/1747091 0601038693

Baldo, J. V., Paulraj, S. R., Curran, B. C., & Dronkers, N. F. (2015). Impaired reasoning and problem-solving in individuals with language impairment due to aphasia or language delay. *Frontiers in Psychology*, *6*, 1523. doi: 10.3389/fpsyg.2015.01523

Bartha, L., & Benke, T. (2003). Acute conduction aphasia: An analysis of 20 cases. *Brain and Language*, *85*(1), 93–108. 10.1016/S0093-934X(02)00502-3

Beeman M. J. (2005). Bilateral brain processes for comprehending natural language. *Trends in Cognitive Science*, *9*, 512–518. doi: 10.1016/j.tics.2005.09.009

Blank, S., Bird, H., Turkheimer. F., & Wise, R. (2003). Speech production after stroke: The role of the right pars opercularis. *Annuals of Neurology*, *54*(3), 310–320. doi: 10.1002/ana.10656. PMID: 12953263

Buchsbaum, B. R., Baldo, J., Okada, K., Berman, K. F., Dronkers, N., D'Esposito, M., & Hickok, G. (2011). Conduction aphasia, sensory-motor integration, and phonological short-term memory – an aggregate analysis of lesion and fMRI data. *Brain and Language*, *119*(3), 119–128. 10.1016/j.bandl.2010.12.001

Butterworth, B. (1979). Hesitation and the production of verbal paraphasias and neologisms in jargon aphasia. *Brain and Language*, *8*(2), 133–161. 10.1016/0093-934X(79)90046-4

Cheang, H. & Pell, M. (2006). A study of humour and communicative intention following right hemisphere stroke. *Clinical Linguistics & Phonetics*, *20*(6), 447–462. doi: 10.1080/02699200500135684

Davie, G. L., Hutcheson, K. A., Barringer, D. A., Weinberg, J. S., & Lewin, J. S. (2009). Aphasia in patients after brain tumour resection. *Aphasiology*, *23*(9), 1196–1206. 10.1080/02687030802436900

Goodglass, H. (1992). Diagnosis of conduction aphasia. In S. E. Kohn (ed.), *Conduction Aphasia*. Hillsdale, NJ: Lawrence Erlbaum Associates. pp. 39–49.

Gorno-Tempini, M. L., Hillis, A. E., Weintraub, S., Kertesz, A., Mendez, M., Cappa, S. F., Ogar, J. M., Rohrer, J. D., Black, S., Boeve, B. F., Manes, F., Dronkers, N. F., Vandenberghe, R., Rascovsky, K., Patterson, K., Miller, B. L., Knopman, D. S., Hodges, J. R., Mesulam, M. M., & Grossman, M. (2011). Classification of primary progressive aphasia and its variants. *Neurology*, *76*(11), 1006–1014. 10.1212/WNL.0b013e31821103e6

Jefferies, E., & Lambon Ralph, M. A. (2006). Semantic impairment in stroke aphasia versus semantic dementia: A case-series comparison. *Brain*, *129*(8), 2132–2147. 10.1093/brain/awl153

Knopman, D. S., & Roberts, R. O. (2011). Estimating the number of persons with frontotemporal lobar degeneration in the US population. *Journal of Molecular Neuroscience*, *45*(3), 330–335. 10.1007/s12031-011-9538-y

Kuperberg, G. R., Caplan, D., Sitnikova, T., Eddy, M., & Holcomb, P. J. (2006). Neural correlates of processing syntactic, semantic, and thematic relationships in sentences. *Language and Cognitive Processes*, *21*(5), 489–530. 10.1080/01690960500094279

Lundgren, K., & Brownell, H. (2016). Figurative language deficits associated with right hemisphere disorder. *Perspectives of the ASHA Special Interest Groups*, *1*(2), 66–81. doi: 10.1044/persp1.SIG2.66

Mahendra, N. (2012). The logopenic variant of primary progressive aphasia: Effects on linguistic communication. *Perspectives on Gerontology*, *17*(2), 50–59. doi: 10.1044/gero17.2.50

Marshall, C. R., Hardy, C. J. D., Volkmer, A., Russell, L. L., Bond, R. L., Fletcher, P. D., Clark, C. N., Mummery, C. J., Schott, J. M., Rossor, M. N., Fox, N. C., Crutch, S. J., Rohrer, J. D., & Warren, J. D. (2018). Primary progressive aphasia: A clinical approach. *Journal of Neurology*, *265*(6), 1474–1490. 10.1007/s00415-018-8762-6

Marshall, J. (2006). Jargon aphasia: What have we learned? *Aphasiology*, *20*(6), 387–410. doi: 10.1080/02687030500489946

Marshall, J., Pring, T., Chiat, S., & Robson, J. (1996). Calling a salad a federation: An investigation of semantic jargon. Part 1—nouns. *Journal of Neurolinguistics*, *9*(4), 237–250. 10.1016/S0911-6044(97)82796-0

Marshall, J., Robson, J., Pring, T., & Chiat, S. (1998). Why does monitoring fail in jargon aphasia? Comprehension, judgment, and therapy evidence. *Brain and Language*, *63*(1), 79–107. 10.1006/brln.1997.1936

Mesulam, M. (1982). Slowly progressive aphasia without generalized dementia. *Annals of Neurology*, *11*(6), 592–598. 10.1002/ana.410110607

Murray, L., & Mayer, J. (2017). Extralinguistic cognitive consideration in aphasia management. In I. Papathanasiou & P. Coppens (eds), *Aphasia and*

Related Neurogenic Communication Disorders (Second Edition) Burlington, MA: Jones & Bartlett Learning.

Nishio, S., Takemura, N., Ikai, Y., & Baba, T. (2004). Sensory aphasia after closed head injury. *Journal of Clinical Neuroscience, 11*(4), 442–444. 10.1016/j.jocn.2003.04.006

Pilkington, E., Sage, K., Saddy, J. D., & Robson, H. (2019). What can repetition, reading and naming tell us about jargon aphasia? *Journal of Neurolinguistics, 49*, 45–56. 10.1016/j.jneuroling.2018.08.003

Purcell, R., Lambon Ralph, M. A., & Sage, K. (2019). Investigating the language, cognition and self-monitoring abilities of speakers with jargon output. *Aphasiology, 33*(9), 1095–1113. 10.1080/02687038.2018.1532070

Robson, J., Pring, T., Marshall, J., & Chiat, S. (2003). Phoneme frequency effects in jargon aphasia: A phonological investigation of nonword errors. *Brain and Language, 85*(1), 109–124. 10.1016/S0093-934X(02)00503-5

Sampson, M., & Faroqi-Shah, Y. (2011). Investigation of self-monitoring in fluent aphasia with jargon. *Aphasiology, 25*(4), 505–528. 10.1080/02687038.2010.523471

Sherratt S., & Bryan K. (2012). Discourse production after right brain damage: Gaining a comprehensive picture using a multi-level processing model. *Journal of Neurolinguistics, 25*, 213–239. 10.1016/j.jneuroling.2012.01.001

Vargha-Khadem, F., Carr, L., Isaacs, E., Brett, E., Adams, C. & Mishkin, M. (1997). Onset of speech after left hemispherectomy in a nine-year-old boy. *Brain, 120*, 159–182. doi: 10.1093/brain/120.1.159. PMID: 9055805

Varley, R. (2014). Reason without much language. *Language Sciences, 46*, 232–244. 10.1016/j.langsci.2014.06.012

Varley, R. A., Klessinger, N. J., Romanowski, C. A., & Siegal, M. (2005). Agrammatic but numerate. *Proceedings of the National Academy of Sciences of the United States of America, 102*(9), 3519–3524. 10.1073/pnas.0407470102

Weinstein, E. (1981). Behavioural aspects of jargonaphasia. In J. Brown (ed.), *Jargonaphasia*, New York: Academic Press.

Wright, A., Saxena, S., Sheppard, S. M., & Hillis, A. E. (2018). Selective impairments in components of affective prosody in neurologically impaired individuals. *Brain and Cognition, 124*, 29–36. doi: 10.1016/j.bandc.2018.04.001

3

CAN HE UNDERSTAND WHAT I SAY? COMPREHENSION IN APHASIA

Mr Green had been admitted to hospital two days ago following a stroke. He was doing well, awake, talking, eating, and drinking. There was no paralysis. The doctor thought that his language was fine, but asked me to check, since it was a left hemisphere stroke. I was newly qualified, but already convinced that I wanted to make aphasia my specialism.

I found Mr Green sitting up by his bed. I introduced myself and explained that I was the speech and language therapist. I said that I had been asked to check his language, as this could be affected following his stroke. I suggested that we had a chat, followed by some brief assessments to explore his speech, reading, writing, and comprehension. I then paused and asked if that was OK. Mr Green smiled, patted my hand, and said: "You're a lovely girl. But I can't understand a word that you say".

It turned out that Mr Green had **pure word deafness**. This is an unusual form of aphasia in which the understanding of speech is impaired, in the absence (or virtual absence) of any other language symptoms. Those affected can talk, read, and write. They recognise non-speech sounds, such as a doorbell or a dog's bark, ruling out audiological deafness. The person will also be aware if someone is speaking but will not be able to interpret that speech.

Mr Green illustrates how language skills can dissociate in aphasia; i.e., he shows that one modality can be impaired while others are either fully or relatively intact. He also illustrates how detecting comprehension impairments can be difficult, since his problems had

DOI: 10.4324/9781003382737-3

gone unnoticed up to the point of his referral to speech and language therapy.

Although pure word deafness is rare, comprehension impairments in aphasia are not. Indeed, most people with aphasia have some difficulties with the understanding of speech, even if those difficulties are mild. Mr Green could tell me about his problems with comprehension. This option is less available to many people with aphasia, as they have co-existing impairments in the production of language. The problems of detection are therefore confounded.

I will start this chapter by describing methods used to assess word comprehension in aphasia. I will describe different ways in which the understanding of words can break down. We will then turn our attention to sentences and **discourse**. I will describe how these levels are assessed, and how they can fail. I will end the chapter by considering the effect of aphasic comprehension difficulties on everyday life.

INFORMAL ASSESSMENT OF COMPREHENSION

Most speech and language therapists begin assessment by using informal techniques, often woven into a seemingly natural conversation. When exploring comprehension, an obvious strategy is to ask questions and see if the response is appropriate. Open questions, such as "who do you live with?" or "what do you do for a living?" will be difficult for those who have production impairments. Therapists, therefore, typically use closed questions to explore understanding ("do you live on your own?"), as these only require a yes/no response. Seeing if the person can carry out requests is another option ("could you pass me that pen?"). More subtle signs might be available. For example, the therapist might say: "I see you have some lovely cards", and then observe whether the person picks up or looks at those cards.

These techniques can only hint at whether or not speech is understood. A person may fail to respond to questions or comments for reasons that have nothing to do with comprehension. They may be withdrawn or fed up. They may make errors in their use of "yes" and "no", scuppering their replies to closed questions. They may have problems with the control of movement which will sabotage the execution of requests. Probability also has to be taken into account. Someone responding entirely randomly to yes/no questions with get half correct by chance. Formal assessments avoid some of these pitfalls and provide more reliable insights into a person's understanding.

ASSESSING COMPREHENSION OF WORDS

Tests of word comprehension often employ a picture matching format. The person is presented with an array of pictures and asked to point to one in response to its spoken name. Figure 3.1 shows one item from this type of assessment.

Here the word "belt" has to be matched to the target picture in the presence of foils or distractors. These distractors have been carefully selected. One is closely semantically related to the target (braces). One is more distantly semantically related (shirt). One is visually similar to the target (the picture of the watch resembles the belt). The last is unrelated to the target (clock). There are 40 items in this assessment, all following this format.

What can we learn from this test? The overall score indicates whether the words have been understood or not. As there are five pictures to choose from, a chance score is 20% (8/40), so the score needs to be substantially above this to indicate good understanding of words. When mistakes are made, the error pattern is also informative. If the person selects mainly semantic distractors, this suggests that the words have been partly, but not fully understood. Selection of mainly visual distractors signals a possible problem with picture recognition. Random errors, together with a low overall score points to a severe breakdown in comprehension. In this instance, the person may be understanding very little from the spoken words and simply guessing the target picture.

Picture matching is not the only test format. Synonym judgement is a further technique. Here the person listens to two spoken words and has to judge whether they are similar in meaning or not. So, they might say "yes" if the words mean the same thing, and "no" if

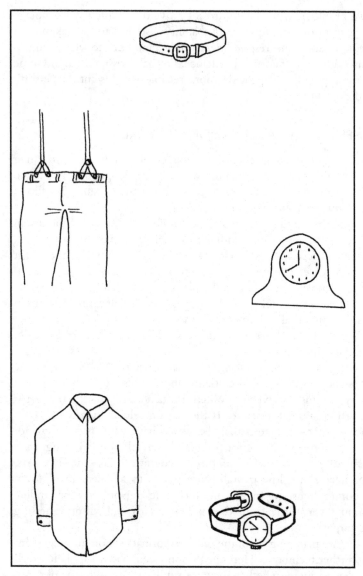

Figure 3.1 An item from the Word to Picture Matching task in the Psycholinguistic Assessment of Language Processing in Aphasia (PALPA, Kay, Lesser & Coltheart, 1992). Target: "belt"

they do not. As no pictures are involved, this task can assess both concrete and abstract words (see examples below):

Concrete word pairs		Abstract word pairs	
Boat	ship	Idea	notion
Boat	flower	Idea	democracy

Success on this task shows that the person can hear, hold onto, and compare the meaning of two spoken words, a skill that may extend to abstract words. On the other hand, failure points to a likely comprehension breakdown.

When comprehension of words is impaired, additional tests can be used to explore the nature of the difficulty. For example, we can use a minimal pair task. Here the person listens to two spoken words. Half the word pairs are identical, the other half differ by one sound. Here are some examples:

mat	map
cap	tap
tome	tome
bed	bed

The person being tested has to indicate whether each pair of words is the same or different. Again, they can do this by saying "yes" or "no". Poor performance on this test suggests that the person has difficulty distinguishing speech sounds, a problem that may underpin the comprehension failure.

We can also see whether the person recognises spoken words, by using a lexical decision task. This uses a randomised list of real and non-words. The person being tested hears each item in turn and has to signal whether it is a real word or not, e.g., by pointing to cards showing a tick or a cross. If they can do this, it suggests that word forms are still retained in their head, even if the meanings of those words are no longer accessible.

Assessing comprehension in aphasia is difficult. When carrying out tests we need to appraise the data carefully and consider possible reasons for test failure. If there were pictures in the test, could the person see all of them? Could they hear the examiner? (often a problem in the elderly stroke population). Were they willing to comply with the test? Above all did they understand what they had to do? Explaining a minimal pair or lexical decision task is not straight forward, particularly when comprehension of speech is impaired. Nevertheless, tests such as these can reveal when the understanding of words is poor and reveal patterns of breakdown.

The following sections describe the test performance of two individuals who showed differing patterns of comprehension failure. The first returns to Mr Green. The second is drawn from the literature.

MR GREEN, A CASE OF PURE WORD DEAFNESS

You will remember that Mr Green pointed out his comprehension difficulties early in our exchange. This enabled me to change tack. I spoke more slowly, sentence by sentence. Where possible, I used gestures to back up what I was saying. Above all, I grabbed a pen and paper and wrote down key words. This enabled me to re-explain my role and invite Mr Green to assessment.

All auditory (spoken) comprehension tests were extremely difficult for Mr Green. For example, he could not match spoken words to pictures or carry out synonym judgements. I decided to modify the test format, by first saying the words and then writing them down. So, with the word to picture matching test, I showed him the pictures and said the target word. In most cases he was unsure of the correct picture or obviously guessed. I then wrote the word down, at which point he confidently pointed to the matching picture. A similar thing happened with synonyms. Once the words were written down Mr Green could judge whether or not they were similar in meaning, even with the abstract pairs.

I wanted to know whether Mr Green could distinguish speech sounds, so tried a minimal pair task. Explaining this was difficult. Again, I used written word pairs, and Mr Green was quick to judge whether these were the same or differed by one letter. However, once he was asked simply to listen to the words, he was very unsure. He tended to judge all word pairs as the same, even when they were not. We carried out the spoken task in two conditions. In the first, I covered my mouth as I spoke the words. This was really difficult for Mr Green. I then took away the cover and encouraged my Green to watch my lips. Now he got some items right.

Finally, I was interested in whether Mr Green could repeat words. I said a word and asked him to repeat it back. He found this very difficult.

He sometimes produced a word that sounded similar to the target, such as "table" for "cable". I then wrote the word down at which point Mr Green was immediately able to read it aloud and explain the meaning ("oh cable, that's for a television or electric heater").

Mr Green displayed clear problems in understanding spoken words. Yet other aspects of language were intact. He could still read aloud and understand written words. In conversation, once he understood the questions, he was able to describe his family, home and working life. He even tried to persuade me to vote Tory (he failed, but not for linguistic reasons). He could write his name and address and provide a written description of a picture.

An obvious question was whether Mr Green was deaf. He and his wife assured me that his hearing had always been good, and I noticed that he reacted to environmental sounds. He was disturbed by the TV on the ward and turned round when there was a knock on the door during one of our sessions. Nevertheless, we referred him for audiological assessment. The results came back as normal.

Mr Green's profile confirmed the diagnosis of pure word deafness. His difficulty with minimal pairs and repetition suggested that he could no longer differentiate speech sounds. Table and cable now sounded the same to him. He was greatly supported by visual cues, most obviously in the form of written words. But lip reading also helped – remember that he coped much better when he could see my lips during the minimal pair task.

Several individuals with pure word deafness have been described in the literature, all exhibiting similar symptoms to Mr Green. Many have bilateral brain damage affecting the temporal lobes of both hemispheres. However, there are also cases, like Mr Green, where the damage is confined to the left hemisphere. Some researchers have argued that the left temporal lobe specialises in processing rapidly changing sounds. Damage to this area, therefore, particularly compromises the perception of speech. If you want to read more see Badecker (2005) for a review of pure word deafness and Slevc et al. (2011) for a discussion of how the left temporal lobe processes speech.

DR O: WORD MEANING DEAFNESS (FRANKLIN ET AL., 1996)

Dr O was a sociology lecturer who had a left hemisphere stroke when he was 60. He initially showed patterns of Wernicke's aphasia, with

Table 3.1 Dr O's Scores on a Synonym Judgement Test

	Spoken	*Written*
Concrete words	35/40	40/40
Abstract words	25/40	39/40

jargon speech and poor comprehension. A year later, his speech problems had virtually resolved, but the difficulties with understanding remained. His hearing was checked and found to be normal.

Sue Franklin and colleagues used a range of assessments to explore Dr O's comprehension abilities. These showed that, as with Mr Green, written word understanding was intact, whereas spoken word understanding was not. The pattern, however, was a little more complicated. To illustrate, Table 3.1 reports his scores with synonym judgements.

When judging written words Dr O made virtually no errors, but with spoken words his performance was much worse. There is a further catch, in that he was particularly poor with abstract words. Remember that this test involves a two-way judgement: you have to say whether pairs of words have similar or different meanings. Thus, with spoken abstract words Dr O was barely above the chance score of 50%. The pattern was the same on all tests. Written words were understood well, whereas spoken words were not; and spoken abstract words were particularly impaired.

There were some further differences between Dr O and Mr Green. When asked to judge minimal pairs Dr O did well. So, he could hear the difference between "table" and "cable". He was also good at lexical decision, i.e., he could detect the difference between real words ("hospital") and non-words ("hopsitle"). The lexical decision test included abstract words, but Dr O still recognised these. Dr O also scored highly when asked to repeat words, even if those words were abstract. In one task he was asked to repeat and define spoken words. There were many instances when he could do the former but not the latter. On these occasions, he was subsequently given the written word, at which point he immediately provided a definition. Here is an example:

> *"soul" soul, soul, soul, I don't know what it is – I should know that. (The written word was given at this point) Oh soul, it's a religious concept, is the soul.*

What was going on with Dr O? Like Mr Green he demonstrated problems with spoken word comprehension in the face of otherwise largely recovered language. But he demonstrated skills that were absent in Mr Green. He could hear the difference between similar sounding words (minimal pairs), repeat words and recognise familiar word forms (lexical decision). However, he was poor at accessing meaning from words, particularly if those words were abstract. Word meanings were not lost, given that Dr O could still understand written words. The disconnection was specifically between spoken words and semantics. Hence this type of difficulty has been termed **word meaning deafness**.

Why were abstract words particularly impaired? The researchers suggest that abstract words have less elaborate semantic representations than concrete words, e.g., because they lack visual and other sensory features. They, therefore, offer smaller and less distinctive semantic targets than their concrete counterparts. So, when access to meaning is impaired, as for Dr O, abstract words are more likely to fall by the wayside.

A final point is worth emphasising. Dr O shows that it is possible to repeat words without understanding them. He could distinguish word forms and reproduce those forms without connecting them to meaning. Clinically, this observation is important. We often have to advise relatives that just because their family member has repeated a word may not signal understanding.

OTHER CASES OF IMPAIRED AND INTACT WORD COMPREHENSION

Mr Green and Dr O had remarkably pure comprehension difficulties, which is rare. Usually, impaired comprehension is one of a range of aphasic symptoms. People with Wernicke's aphasia, for example, often have poor understanding and discrimination of spoken words alongside jargon speech (e.g., Maneta et al., 2001; Robson et al., 2012). In global aphasia, impaired spoken word comprehension is accompanied by severe difficulties in speech, reading, and writing (Munro & Siyambalapitiya, 2017; Barrett et al., 1999).

We also have to be alert to cases where comprehension is relatively preserved. Let's return to Rachel. You will recall that she showed patterns of Wernicke's aphasia, with virtually incomprehensible jargon speech and seemingly low awareness of her difficulties. Given this profile, we would predict that comprehension would be impaired.

However, Rachel performed surprisingly well on auditory comprehension assessments (Marshall et al., 1998). For example, she made just three errors (37/40) when matching spoken words to pictures. She even scored highly on a different version of the task when all pictures were phonologically related (e.g., when "rope" had to be matched to the correct picture, the others being robe and road). Rachel was also good at discriminating real from non-words. In one task she was shown a picture and heard either the correct name or a nonsense word that was created by changing one sound in the target. So, for a picture of a table she either heard "table" or "tibble". Her task was to indicate whether the spoken name was correct or not. Rachel scored well above chance on this test (43/48), failing to detect just two of the non-words.

Rachel clearly retained skills in spoken word discrimination and comprehension. You might be wondering, therefore, why she seemed oblivious to the failings in her own speech. Put differently, why couldn't she hear the non-words in her own production? We were flummoxed by this too. We hypothesised that her difficulties reflected either psychological denial or an inability to carry out the concurrent tasks of speaking and self-monitoring.

INTERIM SUMMARY

So far, this chapter has focussed on word comprehension. I have described how clinicians assess the understanding, discrimination, and recognition of spoken words. Two individuals were presented who had impaired spoken word comprehension, but with subtly different profiles, showing that understanding can fail for differing reasons. In their cases, the comprehension impairment dissociated from other aspects of language. However, this is rare. More typically, poor comprehension is one of many aphasic symptoms, and one that is in danger of being overlooked. Finally, we returned to Rachel and discovered that her understanding of spoken words was surprisingly intact, making her self-monitoring problems all the more puzzling.

Of course, speech is not confined to single words. If people with aphasia are to participate in everyday interactions, they need to comprehend sentences and discourse. The following sections will cover assessment beyond the single word and discuss how comprehension can break down at this level.

ASSESSING COMPREHENSION OF SENTENCES

Understanding of sentences is usually assessed by using tasks in which a spoken sentence has to be matched to one of an array of pictures. The examples in Figure 3.2 illustrate this type of assessment and show how items are controlled for difficulty. These examples are drawn from the Comprehensive Assessment of Aphasia (CAT; Swinburn et al., 2004), which is widely used in clinical practice.

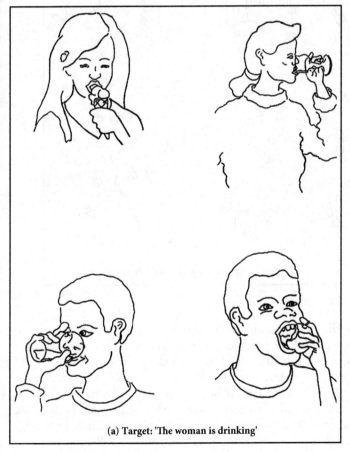

(a) Target: 'The woman is drinking'

Figure 3.2 Examples from the Comprehension of Spoken Sentences Test; (taken from the Comprehensive Aphasia Test, Swinburn et al., 2004)

(b) Target: 'The dancer paints the policeman'

Figure 3.2   (continued)

In the first example, the person being tested will succeed providing they understand the two key words in the sentence (woman and drinking). The second example also calls upon word comprehension, but now the syntax, and particularly word order must also be understood. If not, the person will be unsure who is doing the painting and who is the model. Items such as these are sometimes called "reversible", since they offer the inverse configuration as a distractor (here the target has to be differentiated from the reverse in which the policeman paints the dancer). In most tests complex sentences are also assessed. The CAT version, for example, includes passive sentences, such as "the nurse is chased by the butcher". Other tests include sentences with embedded clauses, such as "Pete saw the cat who was chasing the dog".

Sentence to picture matching tasks can identify the level at which comprehension breaks down. Many individuals succeed with items that purely require word comprehension, such as (a) in Figure 3.2. This skill may extend to sentences with three ("The woman is eating the cake") or even four key words ("The woman is eating the cake with a fork"). Note that these sentences can still be understood purely from the meaning of the words; i.e., providing "woman", "cake", "eating", and "fork" are understood the person being tested will be able to guess the event. However, comprehension may fail the moment that syntax has to be processed. So, with item (b) in Figure 3.2 the person may struggle to choose between the target and the reversal distractor. This was the case for Masie, who we met in the Introduction (see Box 3.1 below). When problems are less severe comprehension may break down only with complex sentences. There is evidence that many people with Broca's aphasia particularly struggle with sentences in which the word order has been flipped (Cho-Reyes & Thompson, 2012). An example is passives, such as "the nurse is chased by the butcher", where the person performing the action (in this case chasing) is positioned after, rather than before the verb.

What makes complex sentences difficult for people with aphasia? One view states that sentence comprehension requires grammatical analysis. The listener has to determine who is the agent of the verb and who is being acted upon. This analysis is more difficult with complex syntactic structures. Another view places greater emphasis on our previous experiences with language (Gahl & Menn, 2016). This experience makes some sentences more predictable, and therefore easier to process, than others. Active sentences, such as "the woman paints the man" are much more common than passives, such as "the man is painted by the woman". Listeners, therefore, typically expect that the first noun in a sentence will be the person (or thing) performing the action. Passives buck this trend, so are problematic. There is an interesting rider to this argument, in that listener expectations are verb specific. Some verbs, such as "elect" are frequently encountered in passive sentences: "he was elected by his constituents/to represent

Box 3.1 Findings from Comprehension Assessments with Masie (Marshall et al., 1993; Marshall, 1994)

We met Masie in the Introduction. She had non-fluent, agrammatic speech, consisting mainly of isolated nouns. Her very occasional verbs were accompanied by no sentence structure. Here is another example of her speech, where she is describing an episode of *Home and Away*:

> *er ... house ... dinner ... nice ... oh yes drinking ... er man ... er police ... oh (Gestures finger wagging) yes*

In conversation, Masie understood simple questions and requests. For example, when asked about her weekend she recounted how she had celebrated Mother's Day which had occurred on the Sunday.

Comprehension tests confirmed that Masie understood nouns well. She scored 37/40 (92%) on the PALPA word to picture matching task. On another test she was shown a picture and asked a yes/no question about its name. Here are some examples:

Picture	Question
Axe	"Is this an axe?"
Parachute	"Is this a plane?"

She scored 98/100 on this task.

Masie's comprehension of verbs was less intact. When asked to match verbs to pictures, she scored 17/22 (77%). All her errors involved the selection of a picture that was related to the target (such as drinking for "eating"). We used the above question task with verbs. Here are some examples:

Picture	Question
A man peeling an orange	"Is this peeling?"
A man pushing a car	"Is this pulling?"

Now Masie scored 84/100. Most of her errors involved the acceptance of a wrong, but related verb.

Masie also struggled with tests of sentence comprehension. We used a picture matching test to explore her understanding of reversible, active sentences. For example, in one item the sentence was: "The policeman follows the fireman". The pictures showed the target, the reversal (the fireman follows the policeman), and a verb distractor (the policeman kicks the fireman). Masie scored 20/30. Nine of her errors involved the selection of the reversal.

It seemed that Masie's production difficulties were mirrored in her comprehension. Verbs were virtually absent in her speech, and subject to misunderstanding. We hypothesised that Masie was not accessing full semantic information about verbs. As a result, she found it difficult to differentiate related verbs, such as "push" and "pull". Sentence structure was also a site of difficulty, and not just in her own speech. When listening to sentences, Masie frequently could not use the word order to determine who was doing what to whom.

Despite her difficulties, Masie comprehended most everyday conversations well. She probably achieved this mainly through her understanding of nouns. For example, when asked "what did you do at the weekend" she could infer the question simply from the final noun ("weekend"). If questions demanded the understanding of word order ("Did West Ham beat Chelsea?") her comprehension was more fragile.

Bolton". With these verbs, active uses go against expectations, so may be more problematic. Returning to aphasia, in many cases sentence complexity affects comprehension. Complex sentences are frequently misunderstood, either because they are more difficult to analyse or because they are less predictable than their simpler counterparts. However, verb specific patterns also play a role. Thus, a person with aphasia may understand 'he was elected' even though this is a passive structure.

ASSESSING COMPREHENSION OF DISCOURSE

So far, we have covered the understanding of words and sentences. The final level to consider is discourse. By this I am referring to more extended uses of speech, for example to tell a story, argue a point or converse. Understanding language at this level requires many skills. Obviously, the words and sentences have to be understood. But we also have to use our working memory to keep track of what has already been said, if we are to follow the plot of a story or a developing conversation. And some aspects of discourse only make sense if we are able to draw inferences or make connections with our general knowledge of the world. Take the following passage:

> Lauren James was full of remorse after her red card. She will miss the upcoming quarter final and is doubtful for subsequent games if England progress.

Those of us who were glued to the 2023 women's football World Cup have no difficulty comprehending this passage. Yet, many aspects of the meaning are only implied, or call upon pre-existing knowledge. For example, the fact that this is about a football tournament is unstated, and the listener has to know that a red card in football involves being sent off and at least a one match suspension.

Assessing discourse comprehension is not easy. Most formal tests employ narratives. In these, the person hears a brief story and is then asked a series of multiple choice or yes/no questions, which probe their understanding of what they have just heard. These tasks have revealed interesting patterns in aphasic discourse processing. Researchers in the 1980s showed that people with aphasia, like unimpaired controls, made fewer errors when questioned on the main idea of a story, than when asked about details (Bookshire & Nicholas, 1984; Wegner et al., 1984). One of these studies also showed that the participants with aphasia understood discourse content, even if it was only implied (see Box 3.2 for details of how this experiment was conducted).

Further research in the 1990s indicated that comprehension in aphasia can benefit from the context provided by discourse (Cannito et al., 1991). This study tested 14 people with aphasia on their understanding of reversible passive sentences, such as "the queen was kissed by the king". Sentences were tested either in isolation or following a brief discourse. In one condition, the discourse provided a predictive context for the sentence, as in this example:

> Many kings and queens were partying in a garden. This garden was filled with visiting royalty. Suddenly a king saw someone whom he loved very much. Soon there was a polite kiss in the courtyard. The queen was kissed by the king.

Box 3.2   Testing discourse comprehension in aphasia

Brookshire and Nicholas (1984) tested 15 people with aphasia on their understanding of discourse. They used narrative paragraphs like this:

> One night Joe and his friend Sam were having a few beers down at the local bar. They were laughing and talking and then, suddenly, they got into an argument and Joe punched Sam. Right away, the bartender called the cops and Joe wound up spending the night in jail. When Sam showed up in court the next morning, he had a bruise on his cheek and a real beauty of a shiner. The judge asked Sam if he wanted to press charges. He thought for a minute and then smiled and patted his friend on the back. "Nope, after all, a guy needs a good drinking buddy."

The person being tested listened to a recording of the paragraph. They then heard a number of statements about the paragraph and had to indicate whether they were true or false. The statements were either about the main ideas in the paragraph, or details; and half the statements were about explicit content (directly stated), while the other half were about implicit content (indirectly stated). Here are some examples:

Main ideas Directly stated:

> Two men were at a restaurant. (False)
> Two men were at a bar. (True)
> The bartender punched one of the men. (False)
> One of the men punched the other man. (True)

Main Ideas Indirectly stated

> The bartender was arrested. (False)
> One of the men was arrested. (True)
> The two men remained enemies. (False)
> The two men remained friends. (True)

Details Directly stated

> One of the men called the cops. (False)
> The bartender called the cops. (True)
> One of the men spent the night in a hospital. (False)
> One of the men spent the night in jail. (True)

Details Indirectly stated

The men's names were Bill and Sam. (False)
The men's names were Joe and Sam. (True)
One of the men got a broken arm. (False)
One of the men got a black eye. (True)

The people with aphasia made more errors on this task than five non-brain-damaged controls. However, in other respects their performance was similar. Like controls, the aphasic participants made fewer errors when statements were about main ideas than about details; and, like controls, they scored similarly for directly and indirectly stated content.

The researchers concluded that people with aphasia deploy normative strategies when listening to discourse. They pay most attention to the main ideas and can equally process information that is explicitly stated or only implied.

Results showed that sentences were understood best when they were preceded by a predictive discourse.

The evidence so far suggests that, in many ways, people with aphasia behave like healthy language users when they listen to discourse. They home in on the key information, rather than details, and pick up content regardless of whether it is explicitly stated or only implied. They also use context to make predictions about what is to follow. However, this is not to say that discourse comprehension is untouched by aphasia. People with aphasia typically do worse than healthy controls on discourse tests, particularly when the stories include complex sentences (e.g., Levy et al., 2012). They also struggle when multiple demands are made. For example, Kiran et al. (2015) show that understanding of discourse breaks down when information is implicit and couched in complex, reversible sentences.

THE IMPACT OF COMPREHENSION IMPAIRMENTS

It is difficult to imagine the experience of living with an aphasic comprehension impairment. For Mr Green, it might have seemed as if even his nearest and dearest were suddenly speaking in a foreign language. Not being able to understand speech isolates the person from conversation and other social uses of language and can lead to misunderstandings and even conflict within personal relationships. Many uses of language for leisure and entertainment, such as listening to podcasts, will be closed off.

Despite these undeniable impacts, there is long standing evidence that those who interact with people with aphasia often over-estimate their comprehension abilities. In a number of studies spouses, professional carers, medical staff, and family members were asked to comment on or predict the comprehension test scores of aphasic individuals known to them (Helmick et al., 1976; Le Dorze et al., 1994; McClennan et al., 1992). In almost all cases the assumed comprehension levels were higher than those actually achieved in formal testing.

This finding is open to different interpretations. It may under-score the hidden nature of aphasic comprehension impairments and raise concerns that, without detection, the impact of those impair-ments will be all the greater. If doctors and nurses are unaware of the comprehension difficulties of their patients with aphasia, this could lead to communication breakdowns on the ward and even negative consequences for medical care. Interactions in the home may be all the more fraught, because spouses are assuming that conversations are understood, when they are not.

The alternative interpretation is less gloomy. Perhaps these interactants are not as mistaken as they seem. They may be responding to the often excellent contextual understanding of people with aphasia. Time and again, we can observe people with aphasia picking up clues in the environment about what is being said. If a nurse approaches with a syringe they will guess that an injection is likely, without needing to follow the verbal explanation. Similarly, the appearance of the physio with a wheelchair will signal a session in the gym. Other cues may be deployed. Research has shown that people with aphasia are highly sensitive to prosody. For example, they can judge the emotion of a speaker from their tone of voice (Barrett et al., 1999; Geigenberger & Ziegler, 2001) and detect the falling intonation that signals the end of a conversational turn (Geigenberger & Zeigler, 2001). They similarly profit from the non-verbal cues that typically accompany speech, such as facial expressions, eye pointing and gesture. This chapter has also described how people with aphasia make maximum use of their retained language comprehension abilities. For example, in Box 3.1 we saw how Masie could guess the meanings of many questions and statements simply by understanding the key nouns.

Once again, we are faced with a seeming contradiction. A person with aphasia may score poorly on a comprehension test yet display genuine understanding of at least some everyday speech. Most probably, this person is combining some understanding of spoken words and sentences with the strategic use of environmental, prosodic, facial, and gestural cues. Strip the message of these cues, and their frailties will emerge. Unsurprisingly, therefore, for many people with aphasia the telephone is a nightmare.

SUMMARY AND TAKE-HOME MESSAGES

The understanding of speech is often affected in aphasia. While this may be the sole impairment, in most cases it will be one of many aphasic symptoms.

Word comprehension can fail for different reasons. In some cases, like Mr Green, there is an inability to distinguish speech sounds. Others, like Dr O, may still differentiate and recognise spoken words, but fail to access meaning from them.

Some people with aphasia demonstrate relatively intact word comprehension but fail when sentences are tested. In many cases, problems only emerge with complex sentences, such as passives. Tests typically use reversible stimuli, such as "The dancer is followed by the queen" to expose the difficulties. These sentences cannot be understood purely from the meaning of the words but require the syntax to be processed.

Discourse comprehension is typically assessed by asking questions about brief spoken narratives. Problems with word and/or sentence comprehension will impact at this level, as will problems with working memory or inference. However, people with aphasia may demonstrate interesting skills with discourse, such as focussing on the most important information and detecting implicit content. There is also evidence that at least some individuals benefit from the context provided by discourse.

Comprehension impairments can have serious social and emotional consequences. However, everyday impacts may be mitigated by the application of comprehension strategies.

REFERENCES

Badecker, W. (2005). Speech perception following focal brain injury. In D. B. Pisoni, & R. E. Remez (eds.), *The Handbook of Speech Perception*. Blackwell Publishing Ltd. pp. 524–545. 10.1002/9780470757024.ch21

Barrett, A. M., Crucian, G. P., Raymer, A. M., & Heilman, K. M. (1999). Spared comprehension of emotional prosody in a patient with global aphasia. *Neuropsychiatry, Neuropsychology & Behavioural Neurology, 12*(2), 117–120. PMID: 10223259

Brookshire, R. H., & Nicholas, L. (1984). Comprehension of directly and indirectly stated main ideas and details in discourse by brain-damaged and non-brain-damaged listeners. *Brain and Language, 21*, 21–36. doi:10.1016/0093-934X(84)90033-6

Cannito, M. P., Vogel, D., & Pierce, R. S. (1991). Contextualized sentence comprehension in nonfluent aphasia: Predictiveness and severity of comprehension impairment. *Clinical Aphasiology, 20*, 111–120. Retrieved from http://aphasiology.pitt.edu/archive/00000135/01/20-10.pdf

Cho-Reyes, S., & Thompson, C. K. (2012). Verb and sentence production and comprehension in aphasia: Northwestern Assessment of Verbs and Sentences (NAVS). *Aphasiology, 26*(10), 1250–1277. 10.1080/02687038.2012.693584

Franklin, S., Turner, J., Ralph, M. A. L., Morris, J., & Bailey, P. J. (1996). A distinctive case of word meaning deafness? *Cognitive Neuropsychology, 13*(8), 1139–1162. 10.1080/026432996381683

Gahl, S., & Menn, L. (2016). Usage-based approaches to aphasia. *Aphasiology, 30*(11), 1361–1377. 10.1080/02687038.2016.1140120

Geigenberger, A., & Ziegler, W. (2001). Receptive prosodic processing in aphasia. *Aphasiology, 15*(12), 1169–1187. 10.1080/02687040143000555

Helmick J. W., Watamori T. S., & Palmer J. M. (1976). Spouses' understanding of the communication disabilities of aphasic patients. *Journal of Speech Hearing Disorders, 41*, 238–243.

Kay, J., Lesser, R., & Coltheart, M. (1992). *Psycholinguistic Assessment of Language Processing in Aphasia (PALPA)*. Hove: Erlbaum.

Kiran, S., Des Roches, C., Villard, S., & Tripodis, Y. (2015). The effect of a sentence comprehension treatment on discourse comprehension in aphasia. *Aphasiology, 29*(11), 1289–1311, doi: 10.1080/02687038.2014.997182

Le Dorze, G., Julien, M., Brassard, C., Durocher, J., & Boivin, G. (1994). An analysis of the communication of adult residents of a long-term care hospital as perceived by their caregivers. *European Journal of Disorders of Communication, 29*, 241–267. doi: 10.3109/13682829409111610

Levy, J., Hoover, E., Waters, G., Kiran, S., Caplan, D., Berardino, A., & Sandberg, C. (2012). Effects of syntactic complexity, semantic reversibility, and explicitness on discourse comprehension in persons with aphasia and in healthy controls. *American Journal of Speech-Language Pathology*, *21*, S154–S165. 10. 1044/1058-0360(2012/11-0104)

Maneta, A., Marshall, J., & Lindsay, J. (2001). Direct and indirect therapy for word sound deafness. *International Journal of Language and Communication Disorders*, *36*(1), 91–106. PMID: 11221435.

Marshall, J., Pring, T., & Chiat, S. (1993). Sentence processing therapy: Working at the level of the event. *Aphasiology*, *7*(2), 177–199. 10.1080/02687039308249505

Marshall, J. (1994). Sentence processing in aphasia: Single case treatment studies. PhD Thesis, City, University of London.

Marshall, J., Robson, J., Pring, T., & Chiat, S. (1998). Why does monitoring fail in jargon aphasia? Comprehension, judgment, and therapy evidence. *Brain and Language*, *63*(1), 79–107. 10.1006/brln.1997.1936

McClennan, R., Johnston, M., & Densham, Y. (1992). Factors affecting accuracy of estimation of comprehension problems in patients following cerebro-vascular accident, by doctors, nurses and relatives. *Journal of Disorders of Communication*, *27*, 209–219. doi: 10.3109/13682829209029421

Munro, P., & Siyambalapitiya, S. (2017). Improved word comprehension in global aphasia using a modified semantic feature analysis treatment. *Clinical Linguistics & Phonetics*, *31*(2), 119–136. doi: 10.1080/02699206.2016.1198927

Robson, H., Keidel, J., Lambon Ralph, M., Sage, K. (2012). Revealing and quantifying the impaired phonological analysis underpinning impaired comprehension in Wernicke's aphasia. *Neuropsychologia*, *50*(2), 276–288. doi: 10.1016/j.neuropsychologia.2011.11.022

Slevc, L. R., Martin, R. C., Hamilton, A. C., & Joanisse, M. F. (2011). Speech perception, rapid temporal processing, and the left hemisphere: A case study of unilateral pure word deafness. *Neuropsychologia*, *49*(2), 216–230. 10.1016/j.neuropsychologia.2010.11.009

Swinburn, K., Porter, G., & Howard, D. (2004). *The Comprehensive Aphasia Test (CAT)*. Hove, UK: Psychology Press.

Wegner, M. L., Brookshire, R. H., & Nicholas, L. (1984). Comprehension of main ideas and details in coherent and noncoherent discourse by aphasic and nonaphasic listeners. *Brain and Language*, *21*, 37–51. doi: 10.1016/0093-934X(84)90034-8

4

IS IT JUST SPEECH? READING AND WRITING IN APHASIA

When the production and comprehension of speech have been ransacked by aphasia, an obvious question is whether the person can still read and write. Unfortunately, the answer is often "no". Brookshire and colleagues (2014) tested 100 people with aphasia on their ability to read words aloud. They found that 68 were impaired. A much earlier study used a wider range of reading tests and found that everyone with aphasia had difficulties (Webb & Love, 1983).

Although both written and spoken language are usually impacted by aphasia, effects are rarely uniform. Writing may be more or less preserved than speech and we have already seen that understanding of written and spoken words can differ. The modalities may be equally impaired, but in different ways. For example, speech may be fluent and full of jargon, while writing is hesitant and restricted to single words. Such dissociations make the assessment of reading and writing essential in aphasia.

When assessing the impact of aphasia on reading and writing we need to know about pre-stroke competencies. This is not straight forward. In a country with a highly developed education system, speech and language therapists can reasonably assume that most of their patients with aphasia were able to read and write before their stroke. However, levels of proficiency will vary. In 2011, the Organisation for Economic Co-operation and Development (OECD) conducted an international survey of adult skills. Findings for literacy in the UK were salutary. Although nearly half the sample demonstrated high level reading abilities, 13.1% scored only at level 1. This indicated an ability only to read basic

DOI: 10.4324/9781003382737-4

vocabulary and extract a single piece of information from a short text. And a concerning 3.3% scored below this level. Writing competencies are likely to be just as variable, if not more so; and even skilled writers may make errors. As an English literate graduate, PhD holder, cruciverbalist, and professor of speech and language therapy, I should score highly in tests of writing. Yet, my unaided spelling is shocking.

Proficiency is not the only source of variation. Individuals also differ in how they use their literacy. One person may find it difficult to contemplate life without the written word. This might be someone who, before their stroke, always had a book on the go, read a newspaper, wrote daily for work, kept a diary and, maybe, even dabbled in creative writing. While for another person, reading and writing may have featured far less in their pre-stroke life. Uses of literacy also change over time. The advent of digital communication, and particularly social media, has arguably triggered a revolution in our use of the written word. Many individuals now conduct a significant portion of their social life through writing. But the form of that writing, with abbreviated spellings, acronyms, and interwoven emojis would be unrecognisable to most 20th-century readers.

This chapter will focus first on reading and then writing. It will describe how reading and writing are assessed in aphasia and discuss patterns of impairment. These impairments arise from points of failure within the reading and writing mechanisms. We will therefore spend some time thinking about how reading and writing are normally accomplished.

READING

The Cognitive Processes Involved in Reading Words

Imagine that you have been asked to read the word DOG. Your first task is to scan and identify the letters in the word, so differentiating it from LOG, DIG, DOT, etc. You need to be able to do this regardless of letter case or font. This tells you that DOG, dog, and dog are all the same word.

Once you have scanned the letters two reading options are available. You might apply a phonological mechanism that converts letters into sounds. This process segments the word into letters, or pairs of letters, that map consistently onto speech sounds, and then blends those sounds to arrive at a pronunciation. Our example yields three phonemes: "d" /ɒ/ (the vowel sound) and "g". Once these sounds are blended, the word can be understood via the pronunciation, much as we understand spoken words.

The phonological reading mechanism has an obvious limitation. It comes a cropper when it encounters an irregular word. This is a word that does not obey the usual letter-to-sound correspondences. English is full of such words, examples being YACHT, MORT-GAGE, and COLONEL. Irish names are another rich vein, such as NIAMH (pronounced "Neeve") and SAOIRSE (pronounced "Sur-sha"). Irregular words would be mispronounced and unrecognised if read via letter-to-sound conversion. They have to be read by the alternative, whole word mechanism. This mechanism recognises the complete spelling of the word and maps it onto the corresponding meaning. If the word is to be read aloud it will also access the whole word phonology.

You might think that the ability to read words as a whole renders the phonological mechanism redundant. Indeed, while reading this text, you are unlikely to be parsing and sounding out the words in the way that I described above. We all, however, fall back on letter-to-sound conversion when we encounter a novel letter string that does not correspond to a known word in our vocabulary. This might be a non-word, such as BLAP, or an unfamiliar name. The well-known actor, Saoirse Ronan, frequently suffers from mangled attempts to pronounce her name via letter-to-sound conversion. You can access amusing YouTube clips in which she reports being called "saucy", "scare-eyes", and "sea-sha".

It is worth reflecting on whether all words are read in the same way. Some research findings suggest that open and closed class words are treated differently during the the reading of text. Let me remind you about this distinction. Open class words are the nouns, verbs, adjectives, and adverbs that convey most of the meaning in language. They are open class because we are constantly adding to their number. I previously gave the examples of "cryptocurrency" as a new noun and "chillaxing" as a new verb. Closed class words include pronouns ("he", "she", "they") determiners ("the"), connectives ("and", "but"), and auxiliary verbs ("he *was* eating"). They play a mainly syntactic role in language and form a fixed group that does not admit new additions. Eye tracking experiments have shown that readers of text typically spend less time looking at closed class words than open class words. Readers are also poor at detecting errors with closed class words, such as omissions or duplications (Staub et al., 2019). It seems that, during reading, scant attention is given to closed class words. On many occasions their presence is inferred, rather than read.[1]

ASSESSMENT OF READING IN APHASIA

Many speech and language therapists begin assessment of reading with a discussion about how the person used reading before their stroke. Questions focus on what they liked to read and frequency of reading. The therapist might also ask about digital media, such as email and WhatsApp. Although addressing uses of literacy, these questions can lead to revelations about competency. For example, I recall one woman saying "I was never a scholar" and talking about how she stopped attending school at 12. Therapists will also ask if the person had any pre-stroke reading difficulties, such as developmental dyslexia. This discussion aims to develop a picture of reading levels pre-stroke and the likely priority given to reading rehabilitation.

After this discussion, I usually ask whether the person has attempted to read anything since their stroke and whether there were difficulties. I might show them some familiar written words for reading aloud or matching to pictures. I typically include some words with irregular spellings to see whether these cause particular problems.

A good place to start formal testing is with an assessment of reading comprehension. The methods used here are equivalent to those employed for assessing the understanding of speech. The Psycholinguistic Assessment of Language Processing in Aphasia (PALPA, Kay et al., 1992) has a written word to picture matching test that uses the same targets and distractors as the spoken test described in the previous chapter (see example in Figure 3.1). In the given example the word BELT (now written rather than spoken) has to be matched to the corresponding picture, in the presence of semantic (braces, shirt), visual (watch), and unrelated (clock) distractors. As with the spoken version, there are 40 items in the test. We are, therefore, interested in the overall score and whether it is substantially above chance (the task involves selecting a picture from five options, so chance is 20% or 8/40). We can also explore the error pattern. For example, if most errors involve the selection of semantic distractors this will suggest that the words are partially, but not fully understood. Given the identical format, we can compare the scores achieved in the spoken and written versions of the test. This will tell us if one modality is better comprehended than the other, or whether both are equally impaired.

As with spoken word assessment, reading comprehension can also be assessed with synonym judgement tasks. You will recall that here two words are presented that are either similar or different in meaning. Here are some examples:

Concrete word pairs		Abstract word pairs	
boat	ship	idea	notion
boat	flower	idea	democracy

The person being tested has to indicate whether or not the words are synonyms by, for example, pointing to cards saying: "same" or "different". In the spoken version of the test the examiner says the words aloud. When reading is being assessed written words are presented. Again, we are interested in the overall score, whether it is above chance (the task involves a two-way judgement, so chance is 50%) and how the written and spoken versions of the test compare. Synonym tasks include concrete and abstract words, so we can explore whether errors are general, or confined mainly to the abstract pairs.

If the person demonstrates good understanding of written words on the above tests, the clinician may go on to explore reading of sentences and more extended text. Methods for this will be described later in this chapter. Conversely, if scores are low, further tasks can be used to uncover the nature of the reading difficulty. These tasks unpick the cognitive processes involved in reading words. Three examples are described below.

Cross Case Matching. In this task the person has to judge whether two letter sequences, in lower and upper case, are the same or different. Here are some examples:

EERGN	eergd
eergn	EERGN

Difficulties on this task would suggest that the early visual stage of reading, when letters are scanned and identified, is impaired.

Written Lexical Decision. This involves a set of written words and non-words. These are shown in random order, one at a time, to the person being tested. They have to indicate whether each item is a real word or not, for example by pointing to a tick or a cross. Problems on this task would suggest that written words can no longer be recognised. Word sets typically include regular and irregular items. This will show whether there is a regularity effect, where regular words, such as MIST are recognised but irregular words, such as WOMB are not.

Reading Aloud. Here words are presented one at a time to be read aloud. Sets are carefully constructed to include regular and irregular words, abstract and concrete words, and open and closed class words. This may reveal patterns in the reading performance, which are informative above which reading skills are retained or impaired.

Difficulties in word reading following stroke have been extensively investigated. This research has uncovered distinct patterns of impairment, reflecting differential damage to the processes involved in reading words. The following section describes some of these impairments. I have used the term **alexia** when labelling these impairments, meaning the loss of ability to recognise and read written words. The term **dyslexia**, meaning the impaired ability to recognise and read written words, is also widely used in the literature.

PURE ALEXIA OR LETTER BY LETTER READING

As implied by the name, in **pure alexia** reading is impaired while all other aspects of language are retained. So, people with this condition can still talk, understand speech, and write.

While not totally abolished, reading in pure alexia is slow and laborious. It is subject to a length effect, whereby short words are read far more quickly, and in some cases more accurately, than long words. Those affected often engage in letter by letter reading, in which they serially name each letter in a word, prior to identifying it. So faced with the word KITCHEN the person may say "k...i...t...c...h...e...n... that's kitchen". Given this strategy, it is unsurprising that long words are so problematic.

Pure alexia is caused by damage in the rear part of the left hemisphere, particularly in the region connecting the lower parts of the occipital and temporal lobes (Roberts et al., 2013). Researchers have argued that this area is home to the "visual word form area", where written words are identified (Leff et al., 2001).

So, what is happening in pure alexia? This is a visual impairment in which whole written words can no longer be recognised, although individual letters can. These letters are fed to the intact language system that painstakingly deduces the word, mainly through the reverse application of writing skills; in effect, the person is asking "what do these letters spell?". You may be wondering why letters can still be processed. This is possibly achieved by the right hemisphere. Cohen and colleagues (2004) investigated a patient called CZ, who had pure alexia following surgery to remove a tumour in the left occipital lobe. CZ underwent functional MRI during a number of reading and letter identification tasks. When compared to controls, CZ showed far greater right hemisphere activation during reading, particularly in the occipital and temporal regions.

There is an interesting rider to the story of pure alexia. For those feeling game, it is described in box 4.1.

GLOBAL ALEXIA

Pure alexia is one of a number of conditions reflecting an impairment in the visual processing of written words. Another is **global alexia**. Here, even individual letters cannot be recognised, with dire consequences for reading. So, people with global alexia cannot name letters or match letters to their spoken names. They also fail on the cross case matching task described above. Despite these problems, letter shapes may still be perceived. LHD was a patient with global alexia studied by McCloskey and Schubert (2014). Although she made errors in letter

Box 4.1 Covert Reading in Pure Alexia

Since the 1980s researchers have shown that some people with pure alexia have covert, whole word reading skills that are not dependent on the letter-by-letter strategy. This was demonstrated through experiments in which words were shown very briefly to letter-by-letter readers; so briefly, that the individuals reported not being able to read the words at all. However, follow up tasks showed that they must have recognised the word. For example, in one study participants were shown written words very briefly, then asked to judge whether the word was the name of an animal or an item of food. Despite professing no knowledge of the words, the participants were surprisingly accurate in making these judgements (Coslett & Saffran, 1989). Another study used a stroop task. In this experiment the person sees a series of written words. They either have to read the words aloud or name the colour of the ink in which they are written. With some items there is an incongruity between the colour of the ink and the meaning of word; for example, the word PURPLE may be written in red. When naming the colour of the ink, unimpaired readers are particularly discombobulated by these items. They take a long time with them and might say the wrong colour, a phenomenon known as the stroop effect. McKeeff and Behrmann (2004) demonstrated that an individual with pure alexia also showed just such a stroop effect. They concluded that she must have rapidly identified the word in order to experience the incongruity between its meaning and the colour of the ink.

How is covert reading accomplished in pure alexia? One proposal suggests that it is carried out by secondary reading skills in the right hemisphere. Another attributes it to impaired but residual whole word reading skills in the left hemisphere. These give the gist of the word, but are insufficient for demanding tasks, like reading aloud.

naming and cross case matching, she performed without error when ask to copy letters. She could also judge whether strings of letters were the same or different, providing they were all in the same case, as in these examples:

FRG-FRG   mrq-mrq
QRF-QJF   pbf-pdf

The researchers concluded that LHD could still see letter shapes, hence her ability to copy and match same case letters. However, she could not identify letters, so could not name them or detect that "A" and "a" were the same. LHD's global alexia was evident several years after her stroke. In other cases of global alexia, letter identification may recover leaving the person with pure alexia.

HEMIANOPIC ALEXIA

When one of the occipital lobes is damaged, for example by a stroke, the person may acquire a hemianopia. This is a blindness affecting either the left or right visual field. Owing to the way that our brain is wired, the affected side is contralateral to the site of damage. So, damage to the right occipital lobe causes a left hemianopia and vice versa.

Hemianopic alexia occurs when there is a right hemianopia, contingent on damage to the left occipital lobe. Here reading of single words is largely unimpaired, but reading of text is not. The problem originates with the eye movements involved in scanning text. Healthy readers of text make frequent, darting eye movements, looking ahead to the upcoming words. With left-to-right text, such as English, the eye movements are to the right. A right hemianopia impairs these movements, causing the textual reading difficulties. Interestingly, people with hemianopic alexia are helped by animated, right-to-left scrolling text (sometimes referred to as "Times Square text"). Reading such text induces eye movements into the affected visual field, and if practised repeatedly may improve reading even of static text (Spitzyna et al., 2007).

NEGLECT ALEXIA

Neglect is a disorder of attention that can arise from neurological damage such as stroke. It is most commonly seen following right hemisphere damage, causing left sided neglect. People with neglect fail to notice things on their affected side. For example, a man with left neglect may bump into objects on his left, may only eat food on the right side of his plate and only shave the right side of his face. If asked to copy drawings, he is likely to omit left sided details, as in Figure 4.1.

Model Patient's Copy

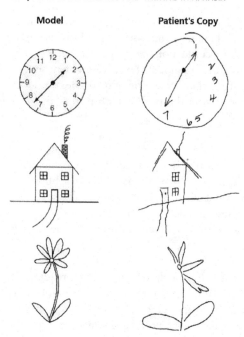

Figure 4.1 Examples of drawings produced by an individual with left neglect

Many, but not all individuals with neglect also have **neglect alexia**, causing reading errors on the affected side of words and text. So, for readers of English, left neglect alexia is marked by errors at the start of words and on leftmost words in text, as illustrated by these examples:

Written word	Response
NEVER	"ever"
ELATE	"plate"
WILLOW	"pillow"

Written sentence: Seven guests came to lunch.
Response: "guests came to lunch"

Right neglect alexia, following left hemisphere damage, causes errors on the right side of words and text. So, for readers of English, word and sentence endings are affected.

So far, I have described peripheral reading impairments that affect the perception of words. Most people with these impairments do not have other language difficulties. In what follows I describe impairments to the central reading processes that decode and interpret script. These commonly co-occur with other symptoms of aphasia.

PHONOLOGICAL ALEXIA

Phonological alexia arises when the phonological reading mechanism that converts letters into sounds is impaired. Whole word reading is retained, meaning that most words can still be read and understood. The condition is identified by an inability to read non-words, such as BLAP. This is because these items can only be read through letter-to-sound conversion. When asked to read non-words aloud, people with phonological alexia typically convert them into real words, for example reading BLAP as "flap".

Poor non-word reading may be the only problem in phonological alexia, minimising the consequences for everyday reading. However, in many reported cases there are additional difficulties. Some individuals also make errors when reading closed class words. As discussed above, these items have low salience for healthy readers, which may make them vulnerable when reading is impaired. Others display phonological problems that extend beyond reading. For example, the person may make phonological errors in speech, such as calling a chair a "char". They may also struggle with phonological tasks, such as judging whether two words rhyme or start with the same sound. This has led some researchers to argue that phonological alexia is part of a generalised phonological impairment.

If you want to read more, Tree and Kay (2006) describe an interesting case of phonological alexia where only non-word reading was impaired. They discuss and challenge the view that this disorder necessarily follows a general impairment to phonology.

Tree, J., & Kay, J. (2006). Phonological dyslexia and phonological impairment: An exception to the rule? *Neuropsychologia*, *44*(14), 2861–2873. https://doi.org/10.1016/j.neuropsychologia.2006.06.006

SURFACE ALEXIA

In **surface alexia** whole word reading is impaired, leading to an over-reliance on the phonological, letter-to-sound, mechanism. A key marker of this condition is a regularity effect. Words which conform to regular letter-to-sound correspondences are read successfully, while irregular words are not. The latter are often regularised when read aloud. For example, COLONEL is read as "Col..on..ell" and PINT is read aloud to rhyme with "mint". People with surface alexia can still read non-words aloud, as these are handled by their intact phonological reading mechanism.

Understanding of words in surface alexia varies. Some individuals not only mis-read irregular words but also misunderstand them. So, the word BEAR is read aloud as "beer" and defined as "a drink". EST who was investigated by Kay and Patterson (1985) was different. Although he could not read irregular words aloud, he could explain their meaning, as these examples illustrate:

THYME	"it grows and smells nicely"
CHOIR	"singing"

It seemed that whole word reading was partially impaired for EST. He could still access the meanings of words, but not their pronunciations.

DEEP ALEXIA

In **deep alexia** phonological and whole word reading is impaired, so error rates are high both with real and non-words. A variety of errors are made with words, including visual errors (reading TABLE as "cable"), errors with syntactic word endings (BAKING read as "baked") and semantic errors (WINDOW read as "door"). Abstract words cause particular problems, as do closed class words. Verbs are also tricky, probably because they tend to be more abstract than nouns. Some individuals with deep alexia can demonstrate understanding of written words (Colangelo & Buchanan, 2007). However, this seems the exception. Riley and Thompson (2010) argue that deep alexia is associated with a general problem with word meaning, affecting comprehension of both written and spoken words.

Deep alexia is a profound reading impairment. Only concrete nouns are read with any success, and even these are subject to errors and misunderstanding.

PAUSE FOR REFLECTION

I have described a number of reading impairments that can arise following stroke. Of these, phonological, surface, and deep alexia are most likely to accompany aphasia. I have argued that these impairments reflect damage to two hypothesised reading routes. One route converts written letters into speech sounds and is impaired in phonological alexia. The other maps whole written words onto their corresponding meanings and pronunciations. This is impaired in surface alexia. In deep alexia both routes are impaired.

This "dual route" account of reading impairments is not undisputed. Some researchers argue that we do not have specialist neural systems dedicated to reading. Rather, they propose that reading is parasitic on general cognitive and linguistic systems, dealing with visual information, phonology, and meaning. The different alexias arise from relative impairments to these systems. So, here is a further instance where patterns in aphasia have stimulated debate about the "normal" cognitive architecture. I will spare you further details, but readers wanting to find out more can consult the following reference:

Woollams, A. (2014). Connectionist neuropsychology: Uncovering ultimate causes of acquired dyslexia. *Philosophical Transactions of the Royal Society B, Biological Sciences.*

READING OF SENTENCES AND TEXT

Most everyday reading activities require us to understand not just written words, but extended text, be it in the form of a recipe, email, newspaper article, or novel. Let's think about what is involved in reading text by using this brief example:

Peter hated driving into town, particularly in the rush hour. On working days, he set his alarm to five o clock, and often delayed his return journey to the evening. Nevertheless, he was usually on the road for at least an hour. By Fridays, he was knackered and looking forward to the weekend.

Understanding this passage obviously requires comprehension of the words and sentences, including instances of slang ("knackered") and idiom ("rush hour"). Working memory is needed, to retain information and make connections across the text. For example, Peter's tiredness, referred to in the final sentence, relates to the long days described earlier. We also have to make inferences. The fact that Peter gets up early in the morning is not explicitly stated but implied by his setting of the alarm. We similarly have to infer that he works in town and drives to work. Some of the inferences call upon real world knowledge. For example, we need to know the typical timings of the rush hour, to make sense of Peter's early starts and late returns.

Given these complexities, we would expect many people with aphasia to struggle when reading text. Understanding at this level can be assessed by asking the person to read paragraphs, possibly of increasing length, and answer questions about the content. These questions take a yes/no or multi- choice format, so that they can be answered even if the person has minimal speech. Sentence level understanding is typically assessed through written sentence to picture matching tasks. These follow the same structure as the spoken tasks described in the last chapter, e.g., where a written sentence has to be matched to one of four pictures.

Despite its importance, reading of text in aphasia has not been extensively researched. Lotte Meteyard and colleagues (2015) investigated the text reading skills of four people with aphasia. All four reported that they could read single words, but were unconfident with longer material, such as newspapers or books. The researchers used a range of assessments to examine the participants' reading and related cognitive skills. These included word and sentence comprehension tasks, paragraph reading, and an assessment of working memory, in which the person had to remember a list of words, both in the original order and in reverse. The results showed that all the participants had difficulty with some aspect of text comprehension. They made errors when answering questions about the content or failed to draw out inferences. These problems seemed due in one case to impaired written word comprehension, and in others to poor working memory. Two of the participants also had impaired comprehension of written sentences.

In a much larger study paragraph reading was assessed in 75 people with aphasia (Webster et al., 2018). Participants had to read paragraphs of varying lengths and complexities, then answer questions about them. These questions either focused on the main idea in the text, or on details; and some questions asked about explicitly stated information while others asked about information that was only implied. A group of 87 controls, with no neurological impairments, were tested on the same materials. The people with aphasia took much longer to read the paragraphs than the controls and achieved lower scores on the comprehension questions. They found questions about details in the text particularly difficult and made more errors when inference was required. Interestingly, their comprehension scores were not affected by the length or complexity of the paragraphs, although the researchers make the point that none of the texts were highly complex, and all were confined to one paragraph.

THE EXPERIENCE OF READING PROBLEMS

We have seen how aphasia impairs reading, both of words and text. What are the impacts of these impairments, from the point of view of those affected?

Knollman-Porter and colleagues (2015) explored the reading experiences of six people with aphasia, via questionnaires, interviews, and observation. All of the participants had difficulties that affected speed of reading and comprehension, and all were reading less often than before their stroke (see quotes below). Despite this, five of the six participants were still keen to read and used a range of strategies to make this possible. All changed the type of materials being read, with a shift to shorter, simpler texts and to materials accompanied by pictures. Many reported using scanning techniques, in which they found familiar words in a text and ignored the rest. The help of others was enlisted by three respondents, e.g., to read aloud or read and summarise a text. One person was using text to speech technology and another was listening to audio books.

Here are some quotes about the participants' reading experiences:

"I have no idea what's going on"

"hard, hard, hard"

"I can't read fast enough to make sense of it"

"But … some word … I don't know that, so … I … leave it out".

Webster and colleagues (2021) consulted a much larger sample ($n = 81$) via a questionnaire. Again, difficulties were highlighted with speed of reading and concentration. Ease of reading was strongly related to the length of the text, with labels and signs being simplest and articles, magazines, and books the hardest. As in the Knollman-Porter study, respondents reported that they were using a range of strategies to facilitate reading, which again included scanning, support from others, and technology. Re-reading, slowing down, and reducing distractions were also reported.

INTERIM SUMMARY AND TAKE-HOME POINTS ABOUT READING

Most people with aphasia have impaired reading. Different types of alexia have been identified, that disrupt reading even of single words. These disorders show interesting patterns of breakdown. Some arise from difficulties perceiving written words. Others reflect impairments to hypothesised normal reading routes.

An inability to read single words has serious consequences for everyday reading activities. Text reading may also be disrupted by associated problems with sentence comprehension and/or working memory.

When people with aphasia are asked about their reading, they report a range of difficulties and a reduction in reading activities. Nevertheless, reading is highlighted as a valued activity for most of those who have been consulted. In the face of their difficulties, many respondents took active steps to make reading possible, with a range of strategies being employed.

WRITING

Witing rarely escapes damage in aphasia. For many (although not all) individuals, it is more impaired than speech. This may be because writing is acquired later in childhood than speech, making it more vulnerable to neurological damage. I will use the term **agraphia** (meaning loss of writing) when discussing writing impairments. The term **dysgraphia** (impaired writing) is also widely used in the literature.

Let's start with two samples of writing. These were produced by individuals with long standing aphasia, who had recovered much of their speech. As you will see, this recovery did not extend to their writing. Both individuals were highly literate pre-stroke and educated to degree level.

The first sample in Figure 4.2 was produced by Ray. He was a retired further education lecturer, but still working as a political councillor. In this sample he was attempting to take notes from a phone message. The transcript of the message is provided.

Ray had a right sided paralysis, so had to use his non-preferred left hand. The lack of clarity in his writing was partly due to this. However, this was not the whole story. Ray had profound problems with writing that extended beyond manipulating the pen. There were virtually no correct words in the sample. Rather, we can see partial attempts at words, such as COM, COMM, and DISC and

'Hi Ray Its Michael Brown here. Thank you for your correspondence and enclosures about the tribunal. I'd like to get your permission to set up a committee to talk about the disciplinary hearing. We need to arrange the agenda and talk about possible compensation. Can you call my mobile phone and suggest a time that would be good for you. My number is 07942 9111321.'

Figure 4.2 Writing sample from Ray (Panton and Marshall 2008)

mis-spellings, such as COMPENATION. Much of the message was left out and there was no sentence or phrase structure.

The second sample (see Figure 4.3) was produced by Stephen, a retired head teacher. He was attempting to provide a written description of the picture (taken from the Comprehensive Aphasia Test, Swinburn et al., 2004).

Stephen had no paralysis, so his writing was much easier to read than Ray's. He achieved a correct written sentence: "The man is asleep", but this was the limit of his success. There were two seeming spelling errors (CAPT for "cat" and TREEN possibly for "trying") and two fragments (CT and M) that were probably failed attempts at further words. The sample is sparse. Most of the detail in the picture was omitted.

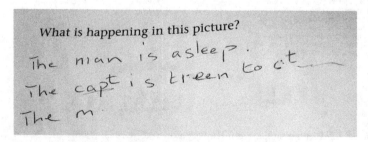

Figure 4.3 Writing sample from Stephen (Caute & Woolf, 2016)

Both Ray and Stephen struggled to write even single words. To understand their difficulties, and the difficulties of others with agraphia, we should consider how the spelling of words is normally accomplished.

COGNITIVE PROCESSES INVOLVED IN WRITING WORDS

As with reading, spelling can be performed via different mechanisms. One option is to assemble a spelling from the word's pronunciation, using sound-to-letter conversion. This might be imagined as the inverse of the phonological reading route. So, the writer segments the word into sounds and maps these onto the corresponding letters. I am sure you can predict the limitation here. As in reading, this route will fail when confronted with an irregular word. For example, if asked to spell "yacht" it would likely come up with YOT and for "mortgage" it might generate MORGIDGE. There is the further problem that many words are **homophones** (different words with the same pronunciation), so map onto multiple spelling options. Take the word "need". If we are working purely from the pronunciation, all of these spellings are possible: NEED, KNEED, KNEAD. Despite its limitations, sound-to-letter spelling is the only option available for writing non-words or unfamiliar words. Faced with a name that we have never met before, we can all have a bash at spelling it, using our sound-to-letter conversion route.

Clearly error free spelling demands an alternative, whole word option. This uses the meaning of the word to access a stored spelling. It copes with regular and irregular words equally well, as long as the word is known to the writer and represented in their written lexicon (a store of all the words in a person's written vocabulary). The whole word spelling route also nails the homophone problem raised above. Here spelling is driven by the meaning of the word. So, if the context is bread making KNEAD will be accessed, if we are writing about a shortfall we will spell NEED, while the source of a groin injury in a pub brawl will call up KNEED.

Writing requires execution, either via handwriting or a keyboard. For handwriting we need to know about the shapes of letters, including upper- and lower-case options, and we need motor skills to write those letters. Keyboard writing either calls upon rapid, skilled motor schema or the "hunt and peck" method of the one finger typist. Both formats require us to retain spelling knowledge, in a short-term memory store, long enough for the word to be produced.

ASSESSMENT OF WRITING IN APHASIA

Of all the areas of assessment, writing can be the most sensitive. Being able to write is often associated with educational attainment and with a person's social or work-related status. Its loss, therefore, may be acutely felt. Writing attempts leave a fixed legacy that confronts the person with their difficulties.

As with reading, I usually begin assessment with a discussion about how writing was used pre-stroke and by asking whether the person has attempted writing since the stroke. I might hand the person a pen and paper and invite them to write anything that they can. Highly familiar targets, such as their own name and address, can also be a good place to start.

Formal writing assessments use picture naming and word dictation formats to explore writing of single words. Targets can be controlled for variables that often affect success, such as whether a word is concrete or abstract, its frequency of use and regularity of spelling. Box 4.2 below illustrates how these factors are manipulated in one set of writing assessments. Non-word writing can also be assessed, to see whether sound-to-letter spelling is still functioning. Here the person is asked to listen to a non-word, such as "brap", and produce a plausible spelling. Copying tasks can be used to evaluate handwriting abilities. Asking the person to change the case of letters, e.g., to convert lower case letters into capitals, can also explore knowledge of letter shapes.

When assessing writing it is important to explore different modes of execution, particularly if handwriting is difficult. Inviting the person to write words on a tablet or computer keyboard may reveal spelling knowledge that was masked in their handwriting attempts. Similarly, they may be able to assemble a word from a set of scrabble tiles, even if they cannot write it spontaneously.

Writing beyond the single word can be assessed by asking the person to describe a picture or provide a written account of a recent event in their life. Tasks can mimic everyday uses of writing, for example by asking the person to write an email to a friend or a recipe.

Box 4.2 Examples from single word writing assessments

The PALPA assessment battery (Kay et al., 1992) includes several writing assessments. Many of these involve writing to dictation; i.e. the tester says a word and the person with aphasia tries to write it down. The words used in the tests are carefully controlled for several variables, such as concreteness, frequency of use, grammatical class, and regularity of spelling. This can help the clinician to detect patterns in the person's writing performance and diagnose different types of agraphia. Table 4.1 gives some examples.

Table 4.1 Examples of stimuli used in the PALPA writing to dictation tests

Stimuli that control for concreteness and frequency of use			
Words that are concrete and frequently used	Words that are concrete and infrequently used	Words that are abstract and frequently used	Words that are abstract and infrequently used
coffee fire school	spider pill funnel	crisis idea length	valour clue satire

Stimuli that control for grammatical word class	
Open class nouns	Closed class function words
situation method truth	therefore anyone maybe

Stimuli that control for regularity of spelling	
Regular words	Irregular/Exception words
bird caravan tiger	lamb soldier yacht

As was the case in reading, distinct patterns of writing impairment have been identified, reflecting differential damage to the normal writing mechanisms. The following section describes a selection of these agraphias.

PHONOLOGICAL AGRAPHIA

This impairment arises from damage to the sound-to-letter spelling route. As a result, non-word spelling is particularly poor. In pure cases, the whole word spelling route still functions, meaning that the person can write most real words with a high level of success.

PR was one of the first people to be described with **phonological agraphia** (Shallice, 1981). When asked to write even very short non-words (such as "bip") he scored just 18% correct. This compared to a score of over 90% correct with real words. PR's writing of real words was not quite perfect. He made frequent errors with closed class words, such as "any", "than", and "with". Words that were poorly understood were also poorly spelled. This was demonstrated in a task in which PR had to listen to a word, attempt to write it down and then provide a definition. When the word was successfully defined it was also usually spelt correctly. However, if PR could not define the word, he also typically failed to spell it. Later studies of phonological agraphia have similarly found that real word spelling is relatively preserved, but not completely so (Henry et al., 2007).

What is going on in phonological agraphia? The very poor non-word spelling indicates that the sound-to-letter spelling route is no longer functioning. The errors with words may indicate some impairment to the whole word spelling route. These may also arise because all spelling, to some degree, requires phonological mediation. Put differently, even when writing familiar words, all of us may make some use of sound-to-letter conversion. Of course, some errors may also reflect pre-stroke competencies. How many of us would score 100% on a test of word spelling?

SURFACE OR LEXICAL AGRAPHIA

RG (Beauvois & Derouesne, 1981) had agraphia following surgery to remove a brain tumour. He was educated to secondary school level, and highly literate before his illness. The researchers obtained examples of his past handwriting, which revealed excellent spelling.

RG was almost perfect at writing non-words, including quite long ones like "ziguno". When tested with real words, his success depended on whether or not they had a regular spelling. With regular words like "madame" (RG was French) he scored over 90% correct. These were words where just one spelling option mapped predictably onto the pronunciation. With irregular words, or words with more ambiguous spellings, his score dropped to 36%. His errors were almost always plausible misspellings. For example, he omitted silent letters, or replaced letters with ones that were pronounced the same. These patterns are illustrated below:

Omitting silent letters:

Target	RG's spelling
Anchois	anchoi
Hochet	ochet

Substituting letters with plausible alternatives:

Target	RG's spelling
Tank	tanq
Photo	fauto
Eglise	aiglise

RG had **surface agraphia**, also termed **lexical agraphia**. Here the whole word spelling route is impaired making the person over dependent on sound-to-letter conversion. This works for non-words and for regularly spelled words. But for irregular words, it often generates errors. As we saw from RG's examples, the errors arise from an attempt to convert the pronunciation of the word into a plausible spelling. Such errors are sometimes described as regularisations. Since RG, numerous other individuals have been described with surface agraphia. Many had lesions in the lower and rear portion of the left temporal cortex (Rapcsak and Beeson, 2004). It has, therefore, been argued that this region stores our memory for how whole words are written.

DEEP AGRAPHIA

Deep agraphia is marked by multiple spelling difficulties. Very few words are written correctly. Attempts may be abandoned or consist of just one or two letters. Semantic errors also feature, for example where DOG is written for the target "horse". Whether or not words can be written is sensitive to several variables. Uncommon words, and abstract words are particularly difficult, as are closed class words. This means that any writing success in deep agraphia is almost entirely confined to common, concrete nouns. Non-word writing is also very difficult. So, a person with deep dysgraphia could probably not generate a plausible spelling for "blap".

The range of difficulties in deep dysgraphia suggest that both writing routes are severely impaired. Sound-to-letter conversion is unavailable, causing the problem with non-word spelling. This also means that the spelling of words is not influenced by their pronunciation, making errors like DOG for 'horse' possible. The whole word writing route is also barely functioning in deep dysgraphia. On many occasions the person is unable to access any information about how a word is spelt, particularly if the word is uncommon or abstract. Sometimes, partial information is available, giving rise to a semantic error or an incomplete spelling attempt.

AGRAPHIA FOR LONG WORDS

When describing the cognitive processes involved in writing I made the point that successful writing involves an element of short-term memory. We have to hold onto our knowledge of how a word is spelt long enough to write it down. In some cases of agraphia this knowledge seems subject to rapid decay. As a result, the person loses sight of how a word is spelt and makes frequent spelling errors, e.g., where letters are omitted, misplaced, or substituted. A key marker of this problem is a length effect. Short words are often written successfully, whereas long words, which particularly tax the memory system, are not. Ray, whose writing sample we saw earlier, had this form of agraphia. We can see him struggling to write the many long words contained in the phone message.

PERIPHERAL AGRAPHIA

So far, I have described writing disorders that affect the person's knowledge about how a word is spelt. Additional problems can affect writing execution. In some cases, knowledge of letter shapes is impaired. Puzzlingly, the difficulty may be confined to just upper- or lower-case letters. For example, the person may still be able to write in capital letters, but make errors in lower-case, cursive script. Other problems affect the movements involved in writing. Here the person knows how letters should be written and may even be able to describe letter shapes. But they struggle to produce those letters on paper. Errors often involve the omission or additions of letter features. So, a "t" may be uncrossed or crossed several times. Peripheral problems with letter knowledge and movement only affect handwriting. If asked to spell using a keyboard, the person should cope well.

ANOTHER PAUSE FOR REFLECTION

Many of the acquired writing problems that accompany aphasia demonstrate interesting patterns, which seem to reflect impairments to one or both of the hypothesised writing routes. As was the case in reading, these impairments have stimulated discussion about the cognitive processes involved in writing and how those processes can break down.

Although patterns of agraphia have been identified, not all individuals conform to those patterns. Stephen, who we met earlier, is an example. Stephen displayed signs of deep agraphia: he had very limited success when writing words and the researchers report that he was poor at non-word writing. However, his sample includes several closed class words (THE, IS, TO) which are typically impaired in deep agraphia. Like many people with aphasia, he defies classification.

THE EXPERIENCE OF WRITING PROBLEMS

A few studies have interviewed people with aphasia about their writing difficulties (Kjellén et al., 2017; Theil & Conroy, 2022). Several themes emerged, which are illustrated in the quotes below. Recovery of writing abilities was described as slow and laborious, with most respondents still experiencing difficulties years post stroke. Many barriers to writing were described, including factors beyond aphasia such as cognitive problems and hand paralysis. Some of those interviewed associated their poor writing with feelings of embarrassment and a loss of self-esteem. Despite the negative feelings, writing was seen as a priority. Almost everyone interviewed was still undertaking some writing activities, for example to maintain contact with family and friends or for administrative purposes. Some preferred written options, such as texting, to using the phone. Writing was also used as a compensatory communication method when speech was severely impaired. For example, one respondent described ordering food in a restaurant by writing their choices. As with reading, many of those interviewed were using strategies to achieve writing goals. These included enlisting the support of others and using technology, such as voice recognition software.

Here are some quotes from people with aphasia about their writing (Thiel & Conroy, 2022)

Slow recovery, and writing is still difficult:

> *"But stroke slow down, improving improving slow hell frustrating"*

> *"my writing is only short […] not like you"*

Threat to self-esteem:

> *"and I feel a bit conscious because fully grown woman can't spell and I think but you have to get over that, but it's very hard very hard"*

Using strategies, such as technology:

> *"honestly it's a godsend … . I can talk to the tablet and it does it for me"*

A RETURN TO MASIE AND RACHEL

Could Masie and Rachel still read and write after their strokes?

Masie's reading comprehension was similar to her comprehension of speech. She understood single words well, but made frequent errors when asked to match written sentences to pictures. Scores on written and spoken versions of tests were virtually the same. On the other hand, Masie's writing post stroke was severely impaired and worse than her speech. For example, she could often say the name of pictured objects, but rarely write those names. Masie's priority for therapy was to improve her speech, so her reading and writing were not extensively explored.

Investigations of reading and writing with Rachel revealed interesting patterns. In the case of reading the picture was gloomy. Rachel's understanding even of single written words was poor. For example, when asked to match written words to pictures she scored just 25/40, compared to a score of 37/40 when the words were spoken. Rachel's writing was also severely impaired, but here there were some hints of preserved abilities. Without help, Rachel could not write the name of any pictured objects. However, there were 15 instances when she wrote part of the name, and four instances when she managed to write the full name when given the first letter as a cue. Remember that Rachel's speech consisted of incomprehensible jargon. She could never say the name of a picture even following a cue. There was another important difference between her speech and her writing. Rachel seemed oblivious to the failings in her speech. She did not attempt to self-correct, and was often surprised or irritated when she was not understood. In contrast, Rachel displayed acute awareness of her writing problems. She crossed out her errors, was frustrated and sometimes distressed by her difficulties. The fact that Rachel could monitor her writing made her willing to work on it, offering a window for rehabilitation. A final assessment gave another positive sign. This used a random set of real and non-words. Each item was shown to Rachel for 30 seconds and then covered up, at which point Rachel was asked to copy it from memory. We counted the number of correct letters in Rachel's attempts. When copying words Rachel managed to reproduce 80% of the target letters, compared to 69% with non-words. The difference between words and non-words was particularly marked with longer items. Here Rachel scored 73% with words compared to 54% with non-words. What do these scores mean? If you or I were doing this task, we would obviously recognise the real words, and would reproduce them easily, using our stored knowledge of their spelling. Non-words would be more difficult. These would not correspond to a real word in our lexicon. So, we would have to reproduce them purely from our short-term memory. Here we might make some errors, particularly with longer items. Rachel showed a similar advantage for the real words. This suggested that she still had some stored knowledge about the spellings of words, and that she was tapping into that knowledge during the task. Once again, this was a positive prognosticator for a therapy targeting writing. We hoped that such a therapy might enable Rachel to write some words which she could use in her everyday communication. I will tell you about this therapy in Chapter 7.

SUMMARY AND TAKE-HOME MESSAGES ABOUT WRITING

Writing is usually affected in aphasia, often more severely than speech.

Different agraphias have been described, that reflect impairments to hypothesised writing routes. In phonological agraphia, the sound-to-letter conversion route is impaired. In surface or lexical agraphia, the whole word writing route is impaired and in deep agraphia both routes are impaired.

Peripheral problems, affecting the recall or reproduction of letter shapes, can also derail writing.

Not all people with aphasia conform to the described patterns of agraphia. Some, like Stephen, defy classification.

When asked about their writing, people with aphasia have reported multiple difficulties that are slow to recover and which may be associated with negative feelings, such as embarrassment. Nevertheless, most of those interviewed were still undertaking some writing activities and saw writing as important. As was the case in reading, many respondents deployed strategies, including the use of technology, to make writing possible.

A FINAL WORD LOOKING AHEAD TO THERAPY

The comments of people with aphasia indicate that reading and writing are valued activities, and therefore important targets for rehabilitation. In other words, therapy for aphasia should not just focus on speech. Therapy may aim to reinstate literacy skills, for example through word reading or spelling tasks; or it may develop strategies that make reading and writing possible despite the impairments. As we saw with Rachel, the written modality may also be targeted as a compensatory communication channel, particularly when speech is severely impaired. We will return to these therapy issues in Chapter 7.

NOTE

1 First of all I apologise for the second use of the revolting "chillaxing". The above paragraph contains a duplication error with a determiner. You may have spotted it. If not, this illustrates how closed class words often fall below the radar. For those needing to hunt for the error, it is in the second sentence.

REFERENCES

Beauvois, M., & Derouesne, J. (1981). Lexical or orthographic agraphia. *Brain*, *104*(1), 21–49. 10.1093/brain/104.1.21

Brookshire, C. E., Wilson, J., Nadeau, S., Gonzalez Rothi, L., & Kendall, D. (2014). Frequency, nature, and predictors of alexia in a convenience sample of individuals with chronic aphasia. *Aphasiology*, *28*(12), 1464–1480. doi: 10.1080/02687038.2014.945389

Caute, A., & Woolf, C. (2016). Using Voice Recognition Software to improve communicative writing and social participation in an individual with severe acquired dysgraphia: An experimental single case therapy study. *Aphasiology*, *30*(2–3), 245–268. doi: 10.1080/02687038.2015.1041095

Cohen, L., Henry, C., Dehaene, S., Martinaud, O., Lehéricy, S., Lemer, C., & Ferrieux, S. (2004). The pathophysiology of letter-by-letter reading, *Neuropsychologia*, *42*(13), 1768–1780. 10.1016/j.neuropsychologia.2004.04.018.

Colangelo, A., & Buchanan, L. (2007). Localizing damage in the functional architecture: The distinction between implicit and explicit processing in deep dyslexia. *Journal of Neurolinguistics*, *20*(2), 111–144.

Coslett, H. B., & Saffran, E. M. (1989). Evidence for preserved reading in 'pure alexia'. *Brain*, *112*(2), 327–359. 10.1093/brain/112.2.327

Henry, M. L., Beeson, P. M., Stark, A. J., & Rapcsak, S. Z. (2007). The role of left perisylvian cortical regions in spelling. *Brain and Language*, *100*(1), 44–52. 10.1016/j.bandl.2006.06.011

Kay, J., & Patterson, K. (1985) Routes to meaning in surface dyslexia. In K. Patterson, J. C. Marshall, & M. Coltheart (eds), *Surface Dyslexia: Neuropsychological and Cognitive Studies of Phonological Reading*. London: Lawrence Erlbaum Assoc.

Kay, J., Lesser, R., & Coltheart, M. (1992). *Psycholinguistic Assessment of Language Processing in Aphasia (PALPA)*. Hove: Erlbaum.

Kjellén, E., Laakso, K., & Henriksson, I. (2017). Aphasia and literacy—The insider's perspective. *International Journal of Language and Communication Disorders*, *52*(5), 573–584.

Knollman-Porter, K., Wallace, S., Hux, S., Brown J., & Long, C. (2015). Reading experiences and use of supports by people with chronic aphasia. *Aphasiology*, *29*(12), 1448–1472. doi: 10.1080/02687038.2015.1041093

Leff, A., Crewes, H., Plant, G., Scott, S., Kennard, C., & Wise R. (2001). The functional anatomy of single-word reading in patients with hemianopic and pure alexia. *Brain, 124*(3), 510–521. 10.1093/brain/124.3.510

McCloskey, M., & Schubert, T. (2014). Shared versus separate processes for letter and digit identification. *Cognitive Neuropsychology, 31*(5–6), 437–460. 10.1080/02643294.2013.869202

McKeeff, T., & Behrmann, M. (2004). Pure alexia and covert reading: Evidence from Stroop tasks. *Cognitive Neuropsychology, 21*(2–4), 443–458. doi: 10.1080/02643290342000429

Meteyard, L., Bruce, C., Edmundson, A., & Oakhill, J. (2015). Profiling text comprehension impairments in aphasia. *Aphasiology, 29*(1), 1–28. doi: 10.1080/02687038.2014.955388

Panton, A., & Marshall, J. (2008). Improving spelling and everyday writing after a CVA: A single-case therapy study. *Aphasiology, 22*(2), 164–183. 10.1080/02687030701262605

Rapcsak, S., & Beeson, P. (2004). The role of left posterior inferior temporal cortex in spelling. *Neurology, 62*(12), 2221–2229. doi: 10.1212/01.WNL.0000130169.60752.C5

Riley, E. A., & Thompson, C. K. (2010). Semantic typicality effects in acquired dyslexia: Evidence for semantic impairment in deep dyslexia. *Aphasiology, 24*(6–8), 802–813. 10.1080/02687030903422486

Roberts, D. J., Woollams, A. M., Kim, E., Beeson, P. M., Rapcsak, S. Z., & Lambon Ralph, M. A. (2013). Efficient visual object and word recognition relies on high spatial frequency coding in the left posterior fusiform gyrus: Evidence from a case-series of patients with ventral occipito-temporal cortex damage. *Cerebral Cortex, 23*(11), 2568–2580. doi: 10.1093/cercor/bhs224. Epub 2012 Aug. 24. PMID: 22923086; PMCID: PMC3792736.

Shallice, T. (1981). Phonological agraphia and the lexical route in writing. *Brain, 104*(3), 413–429. 10.1093/brain/104.3.413

Spitzyna, G. A., Wise, R. J., McDonald, S. A., Plant, G. T., Kidd, D., Crewes, H., & Leff, A. P. (2007). Optokinetic therapy improves text reading in patients with hemianopic alexia: A controlled trial. *Neurology, 68*, 1922–1930. doi: 10.1212/01.wnl.0000264002.30134.2a

Staub, A., Dodge, S., & Cohen, A. L. (2019). Failure to detect function word repetitions and omissions in reading: Are eye movements to blame? *Psychonomic Bulletin and Review, 26*, 340–346. 10.3758/s13423-018-1492-z

Survey of Adult Skills (PIAAC) – PIAAC, the OECD's programme of assessment and analysis of adult skills, Accessed on 9 February 2023.

Swinburn, K., Porter, G., & Howard, D. (2004). *The Comprehensive Aphasia Test (CAT)*. Hove, UK: Psychology Press.

Thiel, L., & Conroy, P. (2022). 'I think writing is everything': An exploration of the writing experiences of people with aphasia. *International Journal of*

Language & Communication Disorders, 57(6), 1381–1398. 10.1111/1460-6984. 12762

Tree, J., & Kay, J. (2006). Phonological dyslexia and phonological impairment: An exception to the rule? *Neuropsychologia, 44*(14), 2861–2873. 10.1016/ j.neuropsychologia.2006.06.006

Webb, W., & Love, R. (1983). Reading problems in chronic aphasia. *Journal of Speech and Hearing Disorders, 48*, 154–164.

Webster, J., Morris, J., Howard, D., & Garraffa, M. (2018). Reading for meaning: What influences paragraph understanding in aphasia? *American Journal of Speech-Language Pathology, 27*(1S), 423–437. 10.1044/2017_ AJSLP-16-0213

Webster, J., Morris, J., Malone, J., & Howard D. (2021). Reading comprehension difficulties in people with aphasia: Investigating personal perception of reading ability, practice, and difficulties. *Aphasiology, 35*(6), 805–823. doi: 10.1080/02687038.2020.1737316

Woollams, A. (2014). Connectionist neuropsychology: Uncovering ultimate causes of acquired dyslexia. *Philosophical Transactions of the Royal Society B, Biological Sciences.*

5

NOT JUST ENGLISH: APHASIA ACROSS LANGUAGES

Much of the literature on aphasia is written in English and is about aphasia in users of English. But aphasia is not confined by language barriers. In this chapter we turn our attention to aphasia in languages other than English and to aphasia in **bilingual** language use. This will tell us more about the nature of aphasia and throw up further insights into "normal" language processing. For example, I hope to show how patterns of aphasia in bilingual individuals help us to understand how two (or more) languages are represented in the brain. We will also consider some important clinical issues. As Britain and other countries become increasingly multilingual so, too, do the caseloads of Speech and Language therapists. We will discuss the complexities of working in a multilingual context and how aphasic clients from diverse language backgrounds can be supported.

CROSS-LINGUISTIC SIMILARITIES IN APHASIA: THE EXAMPLE OF SIGN-LANGUAGE APHASIA

Cross-linguistic accounts of aphasia show not only that aphasia can affect any language, but also highlight the commonalities in aphasia symptoms. Let's take agrammatism as one example. Typical features of agrammatism in English include reduced sentence structure in speech, omissions of inflections and closed class words, limited verb production, and poor comprehension of complex sentences. Some, or all of these symptoms have been described in numerous other languages including Arabic, German, Dutch, Spanish, Chinese, Russian, Japanese, Italian, Greek, Indonesian, and Tagalog (e.g., Anjarningsih et al., 2012; Dragoy & Bastiaanse, 2010; Kuzmina et al., 2013; Sasanuma, 1989; Wang &

DOI: 10.4324/9781003382737-5

Thompson, 2016). Aphasic word finding difficulties similarly pop up in all corners of the Globe. The broad types of aphasia outlined in the first chapter of this book, such as Broca's and Wernicke's aphasia, are applied internationally.

Possibly the most striking cross-linguistic cases of aphasia involve Deaf users of sign language. Research has established that the manual sign languages used by Deaf people throughout the world are fully fledged languages, with their own lexicons and grammars (e.g., see Sutton-Spence & Woll, 1999). We now know that signs are very different from non-linguistic gestures, mainly because they have phonological structure. This is composed not from sounds but from manual elements, such as handshape, location, and movement. For example, the sign MOUSE in British Sign Language (BSL) involves an extended first finger (hand-shape) positioned at the side of the nose (location) and made with a twisting motion of the wrist (movement). These elements are obligatory; changing one results in a phonological error or may shift the meaning to another sign. Unlike gestures, signs can also be combined into syntactically structured sentences. The linguistic status of sign language is underscored by brain imaging evidence showing that sign languages, like spoken languages, are processed mainly by the left hemisphere of the brain (e.g., MacSweeney et al., 2002).

If sign languages are true languages, they should be susceptible to aphasia. This is indeed the case. There are numerous accounts of Deaf people with sign language aphasia following left-hemisphere brain injury. Furthermore, their symptoms mirror those found in spoken language aphasias. Deaf individuals have been described with Broca's type aphasia, involving non-fluent signing and reduced grammatical structure (Poizner et al., 1987; Patil et al., 2014). While others exhibit symptoms of Wernicke's aphasia, such as fluent production, neologistic (non-word or more accurately non-sign) errors and poor comprehension (Corina et al., 1992). People with sign language aphasia have also demonstrated sign finding difficulties and make errors with signs that resemble those in spoken aphasias. These include semantic errors, such as signing BED for chair and phonological errors, where, for example, the sign is produced with the wrong handshape (Corina & McBurney, 2001). If you want to read more Box 5.1 describes Charles, a Deaf man with sign language aphasia (Marshall et al., 2004). Testing showed that Charles's sign retrieval was impaired, despite intact gesturing skills, and uncovered a profile that matched many aspects of spoken language aphasia.

Box 5.1 Charles, a Deaf user of sign language with aphasia (Marshall et al., 2004)

Charles was born deaf to hearing parents. His first language was British Sign Language (BSL) which he acquired at his school for deaf children from the age of five. He worked in a factory with hearing people but socialised mainly in the Deaf community, being a member of several Deaf clubs. When Charles was 54, he had a stroke causing extensive damage to the left hemisphere of his brain. He acquired a right sided weakness and aphasia.

Following his stroke Charles's signing was non-fluent with limited grammatical structure, so showed the patterns of Broca's aphasia. He exhibited manual groping behaviours, as he struggled to recall signs. In conversation he often resorted to gesture to communicate his ideas. For example, he described the hydraulic lift in his bathroom using mime.

Despite his production problems, Charles demonstrated good understanding of BSL. He responded appropriately to signed questions and requests, and performed almost without error on sign to picture matching tests.

Charles's ability to access signs was explored in a series of picture naming tests. In one, he was shown 60 pictures and asked, in BSL, to sign their names. Half the items in the test were rated as highly familiar, such as "car". The other half had lower familiarity ratings, such as 'mouse' (ratings were drawn from a published data base). If Charles was unable to sign the name of a picture, he was usually given a phonological cue. These cues either showed him the handshape of the sign or its location. So, when cuing MOUSE, we either held up a hand with an extended first finger, or pointed (using a pencil), to the side of the nose. The test was administered twice.

Charles often struggled to name the pictures. On the first test administration he scored 33/60 and on the second 36/60. His failures included semantic errors, for example when he signed EAT for KNIFE, and phonological errors, most of which entailed the wrong handshape. His other most common error category involved substituting gestures for the sign. Charles's success in naming was strongly influenced by familiarity. Over both administrations he named 42 (70%) of the high familiarity items compared to just 27 (45%) of the low familiarity ones. His naming was also responsive to cues. A total of 40 items were cued, resulting in a further 15 correct responses. Finally, we were interested in the consistency of Charles's naming. Thirty items were named in both administrations of the test, most of which were high familiarity. Eight items were never named and the remaining 22 were named once or were named following a cue.

What do these data mean? Charles clearly had sign finding problems, that were analogous to the word finding problems seen in spoken language aphasias. Like hearing people with aphasia, Charles made semantic and phonological errors during naming attempts and showed familiarity effects, whereby common items were named more easily than uncommon ones. Anomia (word finding difficulty) in spoken language aphasia is usually interpreted as an access problem. It is argued that words are still available in the brain, but difficult to retrieve. This interpretation sits well with Charles's data. Like many hearing people with aphasia, his naming was responsive to phonological cues. It was also inconsistent, in that many items were named in one administration of the test, but not the other.

A further test compared Charles's ability to employ gestures and signs. The test used 50 pictures of everyday objects. Charles was shown each picture in turn and asked either to sign its name or gesture its use (gestures and signs were elicited on separate testing occasions). Half the stimuli had BSL names that were very similar to the likely gesture. For example, one was CIGARETTE, where the sign involves a V handshape at the mouth (see Figure 5.1). The other 25 items had BSL names that were different from the likely gesture, an example being KNIFE (see Figure 5.1).

CIGARETTE   KNIFE

Figure 5.1 BSL signs for CIGARETTE and KNIFE

Charles's scores showed a clear advantage for gesture. He produced 41 (82%) successful gestures compared to 25 (50%) signs. This advantage was evident even when the signs were similar to the gestures. With these items Charles scored 16/25 in the signing condition compared to 23/25 in the gesturing condition. We asked a group of healthy Deaf controls to gesture the items used in this test. Charles's use of gesture was similar to theirs in many respects. Like them, he often mimed holding and using the target object, and, like them, he elaborated his gestures with facial expressions and extended action sequences.

Charles's results on this second test demonstrated a clear dissociation between the linguistic medium of sign and the non-linguistic medium of gesture. Aphasia, being a language impairment, attacked the former but spared the latter. The dissociation was evident even when the signs were almost identical in form to the gestures. As we wrote in the original paper, it seems that "signs are processed as signs, even when they resemble gestures".

CROSS LINGUISTIC DIFFERENCES IN APHASIA

The similarities between sign and spoken language aphasias are particularly striking, given the obvious differences between these languages. They, arguably, provide the most compelling evidence of universal patterns in aphasia. However, as is often the case in aphasia, we now confront a "yes but ..." Despite the cross linguistic similarities, there are also differences in how aphasia manifests across languages. Here are some examples.

Although agrammatism occurs across languages its precise symptomology varies according to the grammatical properties of those languages. For example, some languages, such as Tamil, German, and Russian have complex systems of grammatical case, marked by closed class words and inflections. Agrammatic speakers of those languages are likely to commit more grammatical errors than speakers of less inflected languages, such as English. Error types may also be language specific. People with agrammatic aphasia typically omit word inflections, for example saying "I walk" rather than "I walked". However, Grodzinsky (1984) argues that this error pattern depends on whether or not omissions are permitted in the speaker's language. English nouns and verbs can shed their inflections and still be well-formed. For example, the plural in "dresses" can be removed, leaving a legal root form ("dress") and we saw above that verbs can be stripped of tense and still be a real word. This is not the case in Hebrew. Here, inflections are woven into the root form of the word and cannot be jettisoned. Grodzinsky (1984) gives the examples of "simla" and "smalot", which translate as "dress" and "dresses". This feature of Hebrew results in a different agrammatic pattern, whereby inflections are typically substituted rather than omitted. So, an agrammatic speaker of Hebrew is likely to use inflected verbs and nouns, but often those inflections will be wrong.

Language differences can also affect comprehension abilities in aphasia. Passive sentences, such as "the cat is chased by the dog", pose a problem for many people with aphasia. If asked to understand these sentences they may reverse the meaning, e.g., interpreting the above example as 'the cat chased the dog'. But difficulties with the passive vary across languages. Ardila (2001) argues that for Spanish speakers with aphasia passives are particularly hard, mainly because this structure is rarely used in Spanish. On the other hand, Bondoc and colleagues (2018) show that speakers of Tagalog (a language used in the Philippines) are better off. This language does not employ active and passive structures. Rather, it uses just one word order with closed class affixes to mark which noun is focussed in the sentence (these are like inflections but come before the relevant noun). So, to express "the cat is chased by the dog" the noun for "cat" is preceded by the affix ("ang") to indicate that it is focused in the sentence. Conversely, to express the "dog chases the cat", the word order is the same, but now the noun for "dog" is preceded by the affix. When Tagalog speakers with aphasia were tested on their comprehension of these sentences they coped best with the passive equivalents.

There are important cross–linguistic differences in the written forms of languages. One relates to transparency, or the degree to which letters consistently map onto sounds. English is an opaque language. It contains numerous irregular written words (such as YACHT and MORTGAGE) with inconsistent letter–sound correspondences. In contrast, many other languages have highly transparent written systems, with few or no irregular words. These include: Spanish, German, Turkish, Greek, and Slovak. We saw in the previous chapter that one reading impairment in aphasia particularly affects the reading of irregular words, that is surface alexia. This alexia is rare (if not absent) in languages with transparent orthographies (see Hricova & Weekes, 2012).

Some languages have more than one script. For example, Japanese uses Kanji and Kana scripts. Kanji is a logographic script, in which each symbol represents a word or **morpheme**; while Kana scripts are phonological, with each symbol representing a spoken syllable. Aphasic reading disorders in Japanese can manifest differently, depending on which script is being read. For example, YT was a Japanese restaurant owner with aphasia and acquired alexia (Sato et al., 2008). When reading Kana scripts YT showed a pattern of phonological alexia, with poor non-word reading and mainly phonological errors. However, when reading Kanji, her profile resembled deep alexia. Now most errors were semantic, and reading was strongly affected by whether words were concrete or abstract, with the latter being particularly difficult. If you want to read more, Box 5.2 describes PF, who had aphasia and alexia following a head injury (Senaha & de Mattos Pimenta Parente, 2012). PF was bilingual in Japanese and Portuguese, so could read Kanji, Kana, and alphabetic scripts. The box describes the subtly different effects of aphasia on his reading, depending on which script he was dealing with.

Box 5.2   PF, Alexia in Japanese and Portuguese (Senaha & de Mattos Pimenta Parente, 2012)

PF was bilingual in Japanese and Portuguese. His home language was Japanese, but he was born and educated to degree level in Brazil, using Portuguese. He worked for a Japanese multi-national company, requiring high-level language and literacy skills in both languages. He also spoke English, although this language was not included in the study. When he was 39, PF suffered a left hemisphere brain injury in a car crash. He acquired Broca's Aphasia and a right sided paralysis.

The researchers were interested in how PF's aphasia affected his reading. PF was literate in four scripts: the alphabetic script of Portuguese, and the Japanese scripts consisting of Kanji, Hiragana, and Katakana. Kanji is a logographic script where each character maps onto a word or morpheme. There are thousands of Kanji characters. A competent reader needs to know between two and three thousand, for example to cope with a newspaper. Kanji is used to write most open class words in Japanese, such as the nouns, main verbs, and adjectives. Hiragana and Katakana are both Kana scripts. Here characters map onto spoken syllables, consisting either of single vowels or consonant vowel combinations. Each script has 46 characters. Hiragana is typically used to represent word endings and closed class words; while Katakana is used to represent loan words (words from other languages that have been adopted into Japanese). The different Japanese scripts engage contrastive reading mechanisms. Kanji is read mainly via the whole word reading route, where the meaning and pronunciation of the word is accessed from each character. Hiragana and Katakana are more dependent on the phonological, letter-to-sound conversion route (or more accurately character-to-sound conversion), whereby the reader assembles the pronunciation of the word from the combined syllables and then accesses the meaning from that pronunciation.

Portuguese is written in alphabetic script, i.e., the same script as English. It is a largely transparent language, in which most letters have consistent mappings onto speech sounds. However, there are some exceptions to this, where letters have varying pronunciations depending on context, generating a small number of irregularly spelt Portuguese words.

PF was given an extensive battery of reading tests across his four scripts. These included reading words aloud and comprehension tasks in which he had to match words to pictures or define written words. He was also asked to read non-words aloud. This was only tested in the alphabetic and Kana scripts. PF's performance on these tests was compared to two controls who were also bilingual in Japanese and Portuguese and had no language impairments.

Table 5.1 below summarises the tasks on which PF was impaired or unimpaired. The former were tasks in which he scored significantly below the controls.

Table 5.1 Summary of PF's reading performance across scripts

Script	Impaired	Unimpaired
Alphabetic Portuguese	Reading irregular words aloud	Reading regular words aloud Reading non-words aloud Matching words to pictures Defining words
Kanji	Reading words aloud	Matching words to pictures Defining words
Hiragana and Katakana		Reading words aloud Reading non-words aloud Matching words to pictures Defining words

Much of PF's reading success could be attributed to an intact phonological reading route, which converts alphabetic letters or Kana characters into sounds. This enabled him to read aloud regular Portuguese words and Japanese words written in Hiragana or Katakana. Non-word reading was also accomplished by this mechanism. In contrast his whole word reading route was impaired. This route is required for reading aloud irregular words in alphabetic scripts and all words written in Kanji. The impairment to this route was not total. You can see that PF could understand written words, including Kanji words that he could not pronounce. The researchers therefore concluded that PF could still use the whole word reading route to access the meaning of words but not their phonologies, or pronunciations. PF also displayed anomia, or a word finding problem, in both his languages. For example, when asked to name pictured objects he scored just 42% correct in Portuguese and 15% correct in Japanese. Thus, he showed a general problem in accessing the phonologies of words, which extended beyond reading.

Once again, patterns in aphasia are informative about how languages are normally represented in the brain. PF's profile suggests that the different languages of bilinguals are processed by common mechanisms. We can hypothesise that PF has one whole word reading route, and one phonological reading route. These routes undertake reading tasks in both his languages, with their deployment depending on the specific properties of the scripts being read. In line with this, his post-injury reading profile can be explained by an impairment to the common whole word reading mechanism, alongside residual skills in phonological reading.

INTERIM SUMMARY

Aphasia can affect any language, including the manual sign languages employed by Deaf people throughout the world.

There are striking cross linguistic similarities in aphasia. Broad categories of aphasia, such as Wernicke's and Broca's, have been described in numerous different languages, as have the symptoms of agrammatism and anomia.

Cross linguistic differences have also been identified in aphasia, reflecting the particular properties of the languages involved. For example, these can affect the types of errors that speakers make or their reading profile.

As illustrated by PF (Box 5.2) cross linguistic differences are particularly intriguing in cases of bilingual aphasia. The rest of this chapter will focus on bilingualism and how aphasia manifests in bilingual speakers. We will see that studies of bilingual aphasia have informed our thinking about how the brain processes more than one language. Finally, I will turn to clinical issues, and how we can meet the needs of an increasingly multilingual aphasia caseload.

INTRODUCTION TO BILINGUALISM

Bilingualism is common. Grosjean (2010), in his book on the subject, quotes survey evidence that over 50% of Europeans can converse in a second language; and he speculates that, in some parts of the World, such as Africa and South Asia, rates are likely to be substantially higher. Levels of bilingualism in the UK were lower, but even here 38% of respondents reported that they used more than one language.

Bilingualism is often defined as high and equal levels of fluency across two or more languages. However most bilingual speakers have varying proficiencies across their languages, usually reflecting different acquisition histories. For example, the first language (L1) may have been learnt from birth at home, while the second (L2) was acquired at school or in later life. Grosjean also emphasises the importance of use, making the point that bilingual speakers often employ their languages for distinct purposes and in distinct contexts. For example, the first language may be used in the home, and the second in the workplace; or one language may be used almost entirely in the written form, while another is only spoken. Such imbalances of use can create surprising imbalances in competence. For example, a bilingual individual who has conducted their working life in a second language may feel unconfident about discussing professional issues in their first.

Bilingualism raises a number of theoretical questions. Perhaps the most prominent concerns the neural representation of two (or more) languages. Put most simply, this question asks whether bilingual language processing employs the same brain regions as monolingual language processing, and whether distinct brain regions are used to represent L1 and L2. Patterns of aphasia in bilingual language users can offer insights here. First of all, we can see whether aphasia in bilingual speakers typically follows left hemisphere damage, as is the case for monolingual speakers. We can also explore cross language patterns. If L1 and L2 are served by common brain areas, brain damage, for example caused by a stroke, should affect both languages equally. On the other hand, if they are underpinned by distinct neural regions, dissociations across languages may occur.

A further theoretical question concerns the involvement of different memory systems in bilingual language processing. Humans are thought to have two long-term memory systems. One is implicit, also termed **procedural memory**. This remembers how to perform activities that have become highly automatic, such as riding a bicycle or playing a musical instrument. The other is explicit or **declarative memory**. This is involved in more conscious activities, such as remembering facts. Both memory systems are thought to play a role in language, with implicit memory underpinning the automatic deployment of syntax, and explicit memory more involved in word learning and recall. Turning to bilingual language use, it has been argued that L1 and L2 make differing demands on the memory systems (Paradis, 1994; Ullman, 2001). L1, which is acquired early and involves highly automatic processing, is particularly dependent on implicit memory. While L2, which is typically acquired later through school instruction is more dependent on explicit memory. As we shall see, this proposal may help to explain some cases of bilingual aphasia.

A third theoretical question concerns the involvement of **cognitive control** in bilingual language use. It is argued that bilingual speakers are constantly exerting such control, for example to prevent them slipping into L1 when speaking in L2. Once again, aphasia may be informative here. For example, we might observe cases of bilingual aphasia in which cognitive control has broken down.

APHASIA IN BILINGUAL LANGUAGE USERS

Numerous studies of bilingual people with aphasia have been reported. Some early cases had right hemisphere damage, stimulating the proposal that language may be bilaterally represented in bilingual speakers. However, as the evidence grew it became clear that in the majority of cases aphasia followed left hemisphere damage. So it seems that bilinguals, like monolinguals, process language mainly on the left side of their brain.

What about the neural representation of L1 and L2? Are there examples of languages being differently impaired following aphasia? The short answer is "yes there are". Fabbro (2001) assessed the language skills of 20 people with aphasia who were bilingual in Friulian and Italian. Thirteen (65%) showed similar impairments in both languages; four were most impaired in their second language and three were most impaired in their first. Box 5.3 has further case examples, illustrating patterns that can arise.

The cases described in Box 5.3 show that languages can be differently impaired in bilingual aphasia. Does this argue for the separate neural representation of L1 and L2? Well, not necessarily. First of all, most writers on the subject agree that parallel impairments, in which both languages are equally and similarly impaired, are most common in bilingual aphasia. Allied to this is the problem of publication bias. Case studies reporting unusual phenomena are more likely to be published than accounts of the typical and familiar. In the context of bilingual aphasia this may have inflated the number of published cases in which L1 and L2 are separately or differently impaired.

A second difficulty is that language imbalances in aphasia may simply reflect pre-morbid patterns. In other words, one language may be more impaired post stroke because it was always used with a lower level of proficiency than the other. Kiran and colleagues (2014) offer data to support this view. They asked ten people with bilingual aphasia to carry out picture and category naming tests. The latter involved naming as many items as possible within the categories of animals, clothing, and food. All tests were administered in both the participants' languages (Spanish and English). In addition to these tests, the participants were asked to complete a detailed questionnaire about how they acquired and used their two languages and were asked to rate their pre-stroke language abilities. A number of factors influenced participants' performance on the naming tasks, but a strong and consistent predictor was their language ability rating. This showed that, across these individuals, word production in aphasia was best preserved in the most proficient pre-stroke language.

The above argument covers cases in which L2 is more impaired than L1 post-stroke. However, it cannot explain paradoxical recovery, where the speaker's first language is most affected by aphasia. These cases might argue for some degree of neural separation between L1 and L2, with the assumption that stroke injury is largely

Box 5.3   Differential patterns of aphasia in L1 and L2

Selective Aphasia

Here aphasia affects one of a bilingual speaker's languages, while leaving the other(s) intact.

AM (Paradis & Goldblum, 1989) had three languages: Gujarati, which was his mother tongue; Malagasy, which is the official language of Madagascar, where he lived; and French, which he learnt at school and used at work.

AM had neurosurgery to remove a cyst in his right hemisphere. After his operation he showed no difficulties in French. However, his family reported problems in Gujarati. These were confirmed in testing, with poor performance in naming, comprehension, and articulation. On the other hand he sailed through comparable tasks in French and Malagasy. Two years later AM was tested again. Now his Gujarati was fine, but Malagasy was impaired, with reduced verbal fluency and syntactic comprehension errors. Happily, testing after four years showed that all languages had recovered.

Differential Aphasia

Here both languages are impaired, but differently so. Silverberg and Gordon (1979) describe two cases of differential aphasia. One of the individuals was a nurse, who was bilingual in Spanish (L1) and Hebrew (L2). She experienced a sudden deterioration of both her languages, owing to damage in the parietal–temporal region of the left hemisphere. Although both languages were affected the symptoms differed. In Spanish, her speech was non-fluent and agrammatic; whereas her Hebrew was fluent, but contained frequent phonological and semantic errors. When asked to repeat words and phrases in Spanish she typically failed, but succeeded on similar repetition tasks in Hebrew.

Paradoxical Recovery

Here a second, rarely used language shows better recovery than the first. A striking case of paradoxical recovery is EM (Aglioti and Fabbro, 1993; Aglioti et al., 1996). EM's first language was Venetan (Veronese dialect), which she spoke with her family and in her work as a vegetable seller. EM's second language was Italian. She learnt this at school, which she attended for only three years. Throughout her adult life EM only spoke Italian two or three times a year, although she did watch Italian TV and read Italian magazines.

When she was 70 EM had a left hemisphere stroke, affecting subcortical structures below the surface of the brain. Surprisingly, after this EM was much more able to communicate in Italian than Venetan.

In testing, her Italian naming was better than Venetan. For example, on one task she scored 97% in Italian vs 50% in Venetan, and a similar pattern was seen in event description (93% in Italian vs 10% in Venetan). She was also much more able to translate words into Italian from Venetan than the other way round. The researchers recorded conversations in which EM was asked either to speak in Italian or in Venetan. EM found it fairly easy to keep to Italian when required, with about 30% of her utterances containing Venetan words or phrases. However, keeping to Venetan was much more difficult. In these conversations over 75% of her utterances were produced in Italian.

confined to the regions supporting L1. EM, who had paradoxical recovery, experienced a sub-cortical lesion (see Box 5.3), as did two more recent paradoxical cases (García-Caballero et al., 2007; Adrover-Roig et al., 2011). Sub-cortical structures are involved in implicit, automatic memory tasks. You will remember that L1 is thought to be particularly dependent on the implicit memory system, and more so than L2. This may be why sub-cortical lesions give rise to the paradoxical pattern, in which L1 is most impaired.

To summarise, aphasia in bilingual speakers usually affects both languages, with parallel impairments being common. When one language is more impaired than the other, L2 typically fares worst. However, there are paradoxical cases in which the first language is most affected, possibly reflecting damage to brain regions that support automatic, implicit memory.

An alternative account for the patterns seen in bilingual aphasia appeals to the notion of cognitive control. Let's recap. We all have to exert a degree of control over our speech. For example, we might edit expletives from our conversation when speaking to an elderly relative, or avoid all mention of the former wife when attending a friend's second wedding. Bilingual speakers pick up the additional need for control over language selection. In other words, when talking in L2 they must ensure that they do not slip into L1 and vice versa.

Controlling the language in which you speak may not seem such a big deal. However, a couple of factors add to the complexity. First of all, there is good experimental evidence that when bilingual people are speaking in L2, equivalent words in L1 are also activated in their brain

(Kroll and Dijkstra, 2002). If this is the case, these L1 words must be constantly supressed for the speaker to stay within the target language. The second point is that bilingual speakers often play about with language selection by indulging in **code switching**; i.e., they import words and phrases from one language when speaking in the other. This might seem like a failure in control. However, this behaviour is constrained by a number of rules, the most obvious of which is that code switching typically only occurs between bilingual speakers who share languages. So, a bilingual speaker will not code switch when talking to a monolingual speaker. Switching also preserves grammaticality. Whole utterances may be produced in the other language or just one or two words. When words are switched, they are most likely to be nouns (see Poplack, 2000). The fact that code switching is under conscious control is also evidenced by the way it is used. For example, speakers may switch for comic effect or because a word in the other language is particularly apt for the context.

So bilingual speakers are masters of control. They can stay within a target language, even though words from the other are resonating in their brain. They can also make code switching detours into their other language, to add fun, colour, or clarity to their discourse; but will only do so when speaking to a fellow bilingual.

The control exerted by bilingual speakers can be susceptible to brain injury. Fabbro and colleagues (2000) describe a bilingual 56-year-old building surveyor who had left hemisphere frontal lobe damage caused by a tumour. Although not aphasic, this individual could no longer control language selection. So, when speaking in his first language (Friulian) he often switched into his second (Italian) and vice versa. This switching was involuntary. It occurred even when he was talking to monolingual speakers or had been instructed to stick to one language. It was accompanied by other symptoms of disinhibition, such as a tendency to tell dirty jokes.

What are the implications for aphasia? Several commentators argue that a breakdown in control may explain language imbalances in bilingual aphasia. It is suggested that the speaker may be unable to supress words in one of their languages, causing the other language to be inhibited. This could lead to patterns of selective or differential aphasia, particularly where the second language is inhibited by the first. Van der Linden and colleagues provide evidence for this theory (2018). You can read Box 5.4 to find out what they did.

Box 5.4 The role of cognitive control in differential bilingual aphasia (Van der Linden et al., 2018)

Van der Linden and colleagues tested 15 bilingual people with aphasia on a lexical decision and flanker task. Seven of the people with aphasia had differential aphasia, with one language more impaired than the other. The others had parallel aphasia, in which both languages were equally impaired. The researchers also tested 19 controls with no language impairments. The controls and people with aphasia had similar bilingual backgrounds.

Let me explain the tasks first. In the lexical decision task, the person was shown a written word or non-word on a computer screen. They had to indicate whether this was a real or non-word by pressing a green or red button. There were 90 items in the test: 45 non-words and 45 real words. The latter consisted of 15 words in the person's first language and 15 words in their second. The remaining 15 were **cognates**. These were words that were the same or very similar across the languages. An example is "wolf" which describes the same animal in Dutch and English. The participants were told to select the green button whenever they saw a real word from either of their languages.

This task assesses word recognition. The researchers were particularly interested in whether there would be an advantage for the cognate items, causing them to be judged more quickly and/or more accurately. This would suggest that both languages are activated in parallel and supporting word recognition.

The flanker task assesses cognitive control. The person being tested is shown a horizontal line of 5 arrows. They have to indicate whether the central arrow is pointing to the left or the right. Items are either congruent or incongruent. In the congruent items all the arrows are pointing in the same direction. In the incongruent items the flanking arrows are pointing in a different direction from the one in the centre. Incongruent items make particular demands on cognitive control. The person being tested has to ignore the direction of the surrounding arrows and focus just on the centre.

How did the participants get on? Lexical decision scores were high, with no differences between the groups; i.e., the people with aphasia coped as well as the controls. All the participants performed best with cognates, again with no difference between the groups. These results confirmed that the people with aphasia retained skills in word recognition. The fact that those with differential aphasia showed the advantage for cognates was particularly revealing. It suggested that both their languages were active, despite one being apparently more impaired than the other.

Scores were also high on the flanker task, but here there was an important difference between the groups. The controls and people with parallel aphasia were over 99% correct on all items, regardless of whether they were congruent or incongruent. Those with differential aphasia, however, had lower scores on the incongruent items. The researchers concluded that they struggled with cognitive control, making it difficult to ignore the contradictory information conveyed by the surrounding arrows.

What do these results mean? The researchers argue that differential aphasia is not caused by selective damage to a language specific area of the brain. This was evidenced by the lexical decision task, which showed that both languages were activated even for those with differential aphasia. Instead, they propose a problem with cognitive control, in which the stronger language is inhibiting the weaker. Loss of control was demonstrated on the flanker test, where participants with differential aphasia were less accurate on the incongruent items.

Time for another interim summary. Bilingual speakers have to exert cognitive control in order to select and stay within the appropriate language for any situation. Skills with control can be affected by brain damage, causing involuntary switching between languages. Differential patterns in aphasia, where one language is more impaired by the other, may reflect control failures. Here a dominant language (usually L1) can no longer be supressed, causing inhibition of the other. Problems with control can be identified with non-linguistic cognitive tasks, such as the flanker test described in Box 5.4.

BENEFITS OF BILINGUALISM IN APHASIA

This chapter has focused on the problems that can arise in bilingual aphasia. You may be wondering whether knowing two or more languages can confer advantages for people who have aphasia. Well, there is some interesting research suggesting that it can.

Lahiri and colleagues (2021) were interested in the impact of bilingualism on recovery in aphasia. Working in Kolkata, India, they recruited a sample of 208 people with aphasia following a stroke. All participants were speakers of Bengali, but 53 used at least one other language (most commonly English or Hindi). Each person was tested twice on a Bengali aphasia assessment. The test was administered for the first time in the week following the stroke. It was then administered again about 90 days later. A recovery score was derived, which was the difference between the scores on the second and first administration of the test. All participants received between eight and ten weeks of therapy for their aphasia between the testing points.

Results were available for 163 members of the original sample, and showed that recovery scores were highest for the bilingual group. Some readers may be wondering if there were important differences between the bi- and monolingual groups in this study, which could have affected the results. If so, good thinking. Sure enough, the bilinguals had received far more education than the monolinguals: a mean of just over 14 years compared to 5.6 years. Given this disparity, the researchers also explored whether education levels affected recovery. There was no evidence that they did. Other variables, such as age and size of stroke were similarly explored, but did not explain away the results. The researchers therefore concluded that being bilingual favours recovery in aphasia.

Where does the bilingual advantage come from? A possible candidate brings us back to the notion of cognitive control. It is argued that the experience of marshalling two (or more) languages makes bilingual speakers experts in control, and that this generally enhances their cognitive abilities. Indeed, if neurologically unimpaired bilinguals and monolinguals are compared on cognitive tests, the bilinguals typically come out on top (e.g., Bialystok et al., 2004). There is even evidence of anatomical differences in the brain, favouring bilinguals (e.g., Li et al., 2014). We have seen that skills in cognitive control can take a hit following brain damage. But if these skills survive stroke and aphasia, they might enhance the effects of rehabilitation and help the person cope with their communication difficulties.

Penn and her fellow researchers (2010) pursued this idea. They administered a range of cognitive tests to nine people with aphasia, two of whom were bilingual. Interestingly, the bilingual participants significantly outperformed the monolinguals on almost all the tests.

Analyses of discourse samples also indicated that the bilingual pair were far more resourceful in their communication than the monolinguals. For example, they used alternative modalities like writing and gesture when their speech failed and called upon external props to get their message across, such as a file of pictures. The researchers argue that their bilingual subjects retained strong cognitive skills and that these enabled them to think strategically about their problems.

So, bilingualism seems to confer cognitive advantages which, if they survive the stroke, may enhance recovery in cases of aphasia. Further advantages may accrue simply from the availability of a second language. Consistent with this view, a number of researchers argue that code switching in bilingual aphasia can be used strategically, particularly to compensate for word finding problems (Muñoz et al., 1999; Lerman et al., 2019; Hameau et al., 2022). So, when unable to think of a word in one language the person may attempt retrieval in the other. If successful this will enable communication to proceed, particularly if the conversation is with another bilingual. Even if not, the switch may be informative, for example because of cross linguistic similarities. In line with this account, there is a tendency for switching to occur when individuals are talking in their weaker language, so allowing L1 to compensate for failings in L2 (Lerman et al., 2019).

This brief review suggests that bilingual speakers with aphasia may be better off than their monolingual counterparts. They may be able to draw on highly developed cognitive skills or use their additional language as a communication resource. I also wonder if their experience of straddling language and cultural barriers is important. This experience is likely to engender skills in flexibility and resourcefulness that are invaluable for overcoming communication breakdown.

CLINICAL PRACTICE IN A MULTILINGUAL CONTEXT

Britain, like many other countries, is becoming increasingly multi-lingual, mainly due to patterns of migration. Speech and language therapists can therefore expect to see a growing number of clients with aphasia who use languages other than, or in addition to English.

When working with a bilingual client the therapist will aim to do at least the following:

- Develop a clear profile of the person's bilingualism; this will include the acquisition histories of all languages, information about how each language was used pre-stroke and about relative competencies across the languages. Patterns of literacy should also be explored.
- The therapist will aim to assess both/all languages to understand the impact of aphasia on each.
- There should be a discussion about which language to prioritise in therapy and reasons for the decision. Ideally, therapy should be potentially available in all of a client's languages.
- Again, in an ideal world, assessment and therapy will be conducted by clinicians who share the client's language and culture, or who have a good understanding of that culture.

None of these steps are straightforward. There are published questionnaires that can be used to explore a person's language background. However, these may be difficult to understand if the aphasia is severe. Assessing aphasia across languages depends on testing materials being available. There are a number of aphasia assessments that have versions in different languages. However, not all languages are covered. If a test is not available, the therapist might be tempted to translate an English assessment. However, all commentators agree that simply translating tests is bad practice. This is likely to result in unsuitable test stimuli, e.g., where naming is tested with culturally inappropriate pictures. Control over levels of difficulty may also be sacrificed, for example because syntactic structures have varying patterns of use across the tested languages.

Perhaps the most challenging issue relates to staffing. In highly diverse settings, such as London, it is difficult for staff teams to reflect all the linguistic communities in their area. In these circumstances, clinicians often have to work through interpreters. I am sure you can think of some of the problems that can arise here, particularly when assessing aphasia. For example, in a comprehension test, the interpreter may re-phrase instructions or add information, so losing control over the materials. When interpreting the speech produced by the person with aphasia, the interpreter may convey the meaning, but leave out important features such as omissions or errors.

If interpreters are not available the clinician may have to rely on a relative to translate. This is far from ideal. It adds to the burden of family members and may distort their relationship with the aphasic person. The accuracy of translation cannot be assured. For example, a family member may iron out their relative's errors when interpreting their speech and rephrase comprehension instructions to make them easier.

So, how can we better meet the needs of clients from diverse language backgrounds?

We can seek to diversify our workforce by training clinicians from a range of language and cultural backgrounds. When there is a large second language community in an area, teams may also employ bilingual co-workers. These are assistant staff with relevant second language skills who can support the assessment and treatment of clients in languages other than English.

More diverse recruitment will not obviate the need for interpreters. Even a multilingual therapy team will confront clients who do not speak their languages. But here too we can make improvements. Most therapists aim to spend time with an interpreter before a session explaining what is about to happen and discussing their role. They will stress the need for exact translation, so that the therapist can understand *how* the person with aphasia communicates and not just what they are saying. The need to translate errors will also be stressed. The therapist and interpreter might rehearse a comprehension task, to ensure that the interpreter is not providing unwitting cues or altering the complexity of the language. Ideally, the therapist and interpreter will have a de-briefing after the session, so that the interpreter can pass on any further observations about the client's language.

Although family members should not be used as interpreters they can act as informants. For example, the clinician can consult them about the language background of the client and seek their observations about his/her current difficulties. Relatives may also provide invaluable insights into the culture of their community. Along with the client, they should be included in discussions about therapy priorities and which language to treat.

We need to increase the availability of assessment and therapy materials in languages other than English. An early resource was the

Bilingual Aphasia Test (BAT; Paradis, 2011). The BAT contains 32 sub-tests covering a range of language skills, such as word retrieval, sentence production, and repetition. Versions of the BAT now exist in over 60 languages. Another example is the Comprehensive Aphasia Test which has been adapted for use in over ten different European languages (Fyndanis et al., 2017). Further adaptations of tests will hopefully increase the range of languages covered and ensure that people with aphasia are assessed with culturally appropriate materials. Adapted tests should have control data, collected from the relevant language community, so that people with aphasia can be compared to unimpaired users of their language.

Finally, we need more research into the treatment of bilingual aphasia. For example, we need to understand which treatment methods work best and what gains can be expected. One interesting strand of research has investigated whether treatment in one language brings about improvements in the other. Although findings have varied, there is some encouraging evidence of cross over effects (Ansaldo & Saidi, 2014). Those who have not been exhausted by this chapter may like to read Box 5.5, describing one such therapy experiment.

Box 5.5 Treatment in Bilingual Aphasia (Croft et al., 2011)

In this study, we were interested in whether word finding difficulties in bilingual aphasia could be improved with therapy. We wondered if both languages would benefit and whether there would be cross-over effects; i.e., we investigated whether working on one language benefited the other.

The study involved five people with aphasia who were bilingual in Bengali and English. All bar one rated themselves as Bengali dominant pre-stroke. They all had word finding difficulties in both their languages that they were keen to work on in therapy.

Each person received two episodes of therapy, one in Bengali the other in English. During each episode they carried out therapy exercises with 60 words. With half the words the exercises focused on meaning. For example, participants were asked to think of words in response to a definition or answer questions about the function of a word ("can you kick a football?"). With the other 30 words the exercises focussed on phonology (or pronunciation). For example, participants were asked to repeat the word, or judge whether it rhymed with another word (*picture of a carrot:* "does this rhyme with parrot"?).

Before, during and after therapy we asked each participant to complete a picture naming test. They had to name 150 words in Bengali, and the 150 translation equivalents in English. Sixty of these words were treated in Bengali, and 60 were treated in English. The remaining 30 words were untreated. This test aimed to find out if word production was improved by therapy.

When this study was conducted there was only one Bengali speaking speech and language therapist in the UK, who lived and worked outside London. We therefore had to recruit three bilingual co-workers who could carry out the assessment and therapy tasks in Bengali. These were undergraduate students from our university who were trained and supervised by the lead author.

How did the participants get on?

One person made no gains from therapy, which was disappointing. All the others improved on the naming test following at least one episode of therapy. Gains were made following therapy in Bengali and English. Two of the participants showed cross over effects. So, working on words in one language improved their production of the translation equivalents in the other. Interestingly, cross over only happened when words were practised with tasks that focussed on meaning, rather than phonology. We speculated that this was because meaning is shared across languages, whereas the phonologies are not (the words "potato" and "aloo" mean the same in Bengali and English, but are obviously pronounced differently).

This study showed that word production in bilingual aphasia could be improved by therapy, although not for all participants. Improvements were made in participants' first and second languages. There was a hint that working in one language might benefit the other, although only when tasks focussed on meaning. There was one final implication. The results also suggest that therapy can be successfully delivered by bilingual co-workers working under the direction of a trained clinician.

CONCLUDING SUMMARY ABOUT BILINGUAL APHASIA AND TAKE-HOME MESSAGES

If bilingual speakers acquire aphasia both languages are usually affected, and often equally so.

Interesting cases have been described where the effects of aphasia differ across languages. These cases may argue for some neural separation between L1 and L2.

Patterns of bilingual aphasia have also been explained by the control hypothesis. This argues that differential aphasia reflects the abnormal dominance of one language over the other.

Bilingualism may bestow advantages in cases of aphasia. These may flow from elevated skills in cognitive control, which promote strategic thinking. They may also arise from the availability of a second language. So, if word production fails in one language it might be attempted in the other.

The increasingly multi-lingual profile of society imposes clinical challenges. This chapter described how clinicians are attempting to improve the assessment and treatment of bilingual people with aphasia.

More research is needed into the treatment of bilingual aphasia. There is some encouraging evidence that both L1 and L2 can respond to therapy. Gains may also transfer across languages, particularly when therapy tasks focus on word meaning.

REFERENCES

Adrover-Roig, D., Galparsoro-Izagirre, N., Marcotte, K., Ferré, P., Wilson, M. A., & Inés Ansaldo, A. (2011). Impaired L1 and executive control after left basal ganglia damage in a bilingual Basque-Spanish person with aphasia. *Clinical Linguistics & Phonetics*, 25(6–7), 480–498. 10.3109/02699206.2011. 563338

Aglioti, S., & Fabbro, F. (1993). Paradoxical selective recovery in a bilingual aphasic following subcortical lesions. *Neuroreport*, 4(12), 1359–1362. 10. 1097/00001756-199309150-00019

Aglioti, S., Beltramello, A., Girardi, F., & Fabbro, F. (1996). Neurolinguistic and follow-up study of an unusual pattern of recovery from bilingual subcortical aphasia. *Brain*, 119(5), 1551–1564. 10.1093/brain/119.5.1551

Anjarningsih, H. Y., Haryadi-Soebadi, R. D., Gofir, A., & Bastiaanse, R. (2012). Characterising agrammatism in standard Indonesian. *Aphasiology*, 26(6), 757–784. 10.1080/02687038.2011.648370

Ansaldo, A. I., & Saidi, L. G. (2014). Aphasia therapy in the age of globalization: Cross-linguistic therapy effects in bilingual aphasia. *Behavioural Neurology*, 2014, 603085-10. 10.1155/2014/603085

Ardila, A. (2001). The manifestation of aphasic symptoms in Spanish. *Journal of Neurolinguistics*, 14, 337–347.

Bialystok, E., Craik, F. I. M., Klein, R., & Viswanathan, M. (2004). Bilingualism, aging, and cognitive control: Evidence from the Simon task. *Psychology and Aging*, 19(2), 290–303. 10.1037/0882-7974.19.2.290

Bondoc, I., O'Grady, W., Deen, K., & Tanaka, K. (2018). Agrammatism in Tagalog: Voice and relativisation. *Aphasiology*, *32*(5), 598–617. doi: 10.1080/02687038.2017.1366417

Corina, D. P., Poizner, H., Bellugi, U., Feinberg, T., Dowd, D., & O'Grady-Batch, L. (1992). Dissociation between linguistic and nonlinguistic gestural systems: A case for compositionality. *Brain and Language*, *43*(3), 414–447. 10.1016/0093-934X(92)90110-Z

Corina, D. P., & McBurney, S. L. (2001). The neural representation of language in users of American sign language. *Journal of Communication Disorders*, *34*(6), 455–471. 10.1016/S0021-9924(01)00063-6

Croft, S., Marshall, J., Pring, T., & Hardwick, M. (2011). Therapy for naming difficulties in bilingual aphasia: Which language benefits? *International Journal of Language and Communication Disorders*, *46*(1), 48–62. doi: 10.3109/13682822.2010.484845

Dragoy, O., & Bastiaanse, R. (2010). Verb production and word order in Russian agrammatic speakers. *Aphasiology*, *24*(1), 28–55. 10.1080/02687030802586902

Fabbro, F. (2001). The bilingual brain: Bilingual aphasia. *Brain and Language*, *79*(2), 201–210. 10.1006/brln.2001.2480

Fabbro, F., Skrap, M., & Aglioti, S. (2000). Pathological switching between languages after frontal lesions in a bilingual patient. *Journal of Neurology, Neurosurgery and Psychiatry*, *68*(5), 650–652. 10.1136/jnnp.68.5.650

Fyndanis, V., Lind, M., Varlokosta, S., Kambanaros, M., Soroli, E., Ceder, K., Grohmann, K., Rofes, A., Gram Simonsen, H., Bjekić, J., Gavarró, A., Kuvač Kraljević, J., Martínez-Ferreiro, S., Munarriz, A., Pourquie, M., Vuksanović, J., Zakariás, L., & Howard D. (2017). Cross-linguistic adaptations of The Comprehensive Aphasia Test: Challenges and solutions, *Clinical Linguistics & Phonetics*, *31*(7–9), 697–710. doi: 10.1080/02699206.2017.1310299

García-Caballero, A., García-Lado, I., González-Hermida, J., Area, R., Recimil, M. J., Juncos Rabadán, O., Lamas, S., Ozaita, G., & Jorge, F. J. (2007). Paradoxical recovery in a bilingual patient with aphasia after right capsuloputaminal infarction. *Journal of Neurology, Neurosurgery and Psychiatry*, *78*(1), 89–91. 10.1136/jnnp.2006.095406

Grodzinsky, Y. (1984). The syntactic characterization of agrammatism. *Cognition*, *16*(2), 99–120. 10.1016/0010-0277(84)90001-5

Grosjean, F. (2010). *Bilingual: Life and Reality*. Harvard University Press. 10.4159/9780674056459

Hameau, S., Dmowski, U., & Nickels, L. (2022). Factors affecting cross-language activation and language mixing in bilingual aphasia: A case study. *Aphasiology*, *37*(8), 1149–1172. 10.1080/02687038.2022.2081960

Hricová, M., & Weekes, B. (2012). Acquired dyslexia in a transparent orthography: An analysis of acquired disorders of reading in the Slovak language. *Behavioural Neurology, 25*, 205–213.

Kiran, S., Balachandran, I., & Lucas, J. (2014). The nature of lexical-semantic access in bilingual aphasia. *Behavioural Neurology*, 389565-18. 10.1155/2014/389565

Kroll, J. F. and Dijkstra, T. (2002). The bilingual lexicon. In R. Kaplan (ed.), *The Oxford Handbook of Applied Linguistics*. Oxford: Oxford University Press. pp. 301–321.

Kuzmina, E., Chekmaev, D., Skvortsov, A., & Weekes, B. (2013). Bilingual aphasia in a Mordovian-Russian speaker. *Procedia, Social and Behavioral Sciences, 94*, 32–33. 10.1016/j.sbspro.2013.09.013

Lahiri, D., Ardila, A., Dubey, S., Mukherjee, A., Chatterjee, K., & Ray, B. K. (2021). Effect of bilingualism on aphasia recovery. *Aphasiology, 35*(8), 1103–1124. doi: 10.1080/02687038.2020.1812032

Lerman, A., Pazuelo, L., Kizner, L., Borodkin, K., & Goral, M. (2019). Language mixing patterns in a bilingual individual with non-fluent aphasia. *Aphasiology, 33*(9), 1137–1153. 10.1080/02687038.2018.1546821

Li, P., Legault, J., & Litcofsky, K. A. (2014). Neuroplasticity as a function of second language learning: Anatomical changes in the human brain. *Cortex, 58*, 301–324. doi: 10.1016/j.cortex.2014.05.001

MacSweeney, M., Woll, B., Campbell, R., McGuire, P. K., David, A. S., Williams, S. C. R., Suckling, J., Calvert, G. A., & Brammer, M. J. (2002). Neural systems underlying British Sign Language and audio-visual English processing in native users. *Brain, 125*(7), 1583–1593. 10.1093/brain/awf153

Marshall, J., Atkinson, J., Smulovitch, E., Thacker, A., & Woll, B. (2004). Aphasia in a user of British Sign Language: Dissociation between sign and gesture. *Cognitive Neuropsychology, 21*(5), 537–554. doi: 10.1080/02643290342000249

Muñoz, M. L., Marquardt, T. P., & Copeland, G. (1999). A comparison of the codeswitching patterns of aphasic and neurologically normal bilingual speakers of English and Spanish. *Brain and Language, 66*(2), 249–274. 10.1006/brln.1998.2021

Paradis, M. (2011). Principles underlying the Bilingual Aphasia Test (BAT) and its uses. *Clinical Linguistics & Phonetics, 25*(6–7), 427–443. 10.3109/02699206.2011.560326

Paradis, M. (1994). Neurolinguistic aspects of implicit and explicit memory: Implications for bilingualism and second language acquisition. In N. C. Ellis (ed.), *Implicit and Explicit Learning of Languages*. London: Academic Press. pp. 393–419.

Paradis, M., & Goldblum, M. (1989). Selective crossed aphasia in a trilingual aphasic patient followed by reciprocal antagonism. *Brain and Language, 36*, 62–75.

Patil, G. S., Rangasayee, R., & Mukundan, G. (2014). Non-fluent aphasia in deaf user of Indian sign language: A case study. *Cognitive Linguistic Studies*, *1*(1), 147–153. 10.1075/cogls.1.1.07pat

Penn, C., Frankel, T., Watermeyer, J., & Russell, N. (2010). Executive function and conversational strategies in bilingual aphasia. *Aphasiology*, *24*(2), 288–308. DOI: 10.1080/02687030902958399

Poizner, H., Klima, E., & Bellugi, U. (1987). *What the Hands Reveal About the Brain*. Cambridge, MA: MIT Press/Bradford Books.

Poplack, S. (2000). Sometimes I'll start a sentence in Spanish Y termino en aspanol: Toward a typology of code switching. In L. Wei (ed.), *The Bilingualism Reader*. London: Routledge.

Sasanuma, S. (1989). Agrammatism in Japanese — A cross-language approach. *Journal of Neurolinguistics*, *4*(2), 233–242. 10.1016/0911-6044(89)90015-8

Sato, H., Patterson, K., Fushimi, T., Maxim, J., & Bryan, K. (2008). Deep dyslexia for kanji and phonological dyslexia for kana: Different manifestations from a common source. *Neurocase*, *14*(6), 508–524. doi: 10.1080/13554790802372135

Senaha, M. L. H., & de Mattos Pimenta Parente, M. A. (2012). Acquired dyslexia in three writing systems: Study of a Portuguese-Japanese bilingual aphasic patient. *Behavioural Neurology*, *25*(3), 255–272. 10.3233/BEN-2012-119001

Silverberg, R., & Gordon, H. W. (1979). Differential aphasia in two bilingual individuals. *Neurology*, *29*, 51–55.

Sutton-Spence, R., & Woll, B. (1999). *The Linguistics of British Sign Language*. Cambridge: Cambridge University Press.

Ullman, M. (2001). A neurocognitive perspective on language: The declarative/procedural model. *Nature Reviews, Neuroscience*, *2*, 717–726.

Van der Linden, L., Verreyt, N., Letter, M., Hemelsoet, D., Mariën, P., Santens, P., Stevens, M., Szmalec, A., & Duyck, W. (2018). Cognate effects and cognitive control in patients with parallel and differential bilingual aphasia. *International Journal of Language & Communication Disorders*, *53*(3), 515–525. 10.1111/1460-6984.12365

Wang, H., & Thompson, C. K. (2016). Assessing syntactic deficits in Chinese Broca's aphasia using the Northwestern Assessment of Verbs and Sentences-Chinese (NAVS-C). *Aphasiology*, *30*(7), 815–840. 10.1080/02687038.2015.1111995

6

LIVING WITH APHASIA

When Masie and Rachel acquired aphasia following their strokes their lives were turned upside down. Masie, who was of working age, had to retire from her post in the Civil Service. She lost contact with friends and became more dependent on her husband for many aspects of her life, such as managing finances. Money was a general focus of concern, given the loss of Masie's income. Rachel had retired prior to her stroke, but retained interests in her former academic life and was still in touch with many colleagues. She lived alone in a central London flat and enjoyed the cultural and leisure opportunities that this afforded. After her stroke, she had to relinquish her flat and move into residential care, where she faced almost daily communication breakdowns with staff. She was unable to participate in academic events or read academic literature, and contacts with former colleagues dwindled away. Her leisure activities were also affected. Travelling to concerts and shows was problematic and her language difficulties made books, films, plays, television and talk radio difficult to follow. More positively, Rachel had the support of two loyal friends. They visited regularly, took her to parks and exhibitions and included her in foreign holidays. Masie was sustained by the love and support of her family. She also relished her involvement in a university based aphasia group.

This chapter will discuss the impacts of aphasia on people's lives. Much of the story is gloomy. As we saw with Masie and Rachel, aphasia is associated with profound social and personal losses that can wreak havoc on quality of life. In most cases, the effects are also felt by family members. Despite this, people can live successfully with aphasia, and factors have been identified that help to achieve this outcome.

DOI: 10.4324/9781003382737-6

I will start by discussing some of the research methods that have been used to explore these issues. How do you capture the experiences of people with aphasia, given that their capacity to report those experiences is profoundly affected by the condition?

RESEARCH METHODS

If you want to know how a person feels about a particular situation, the obvious thing to do is ask them. Unsurprisingly, this is the main approach taken in aphasia research, albeit using sophisticated methods of asking. These methods try to ensure that the question is understood, and that the person with aphasia has a means to reply.

One way of asking is via questionnaires. These use a fixed set of carefully worded questions that are typically answered though multiple choice options or rating scales. A good example is the Stroke and Aphasia Quality of Life Scale – 39 (SAQOL-39; Hilari et al, 2003). This comprises 39 questions that ask about physical functioning, communication and psycho-social aspects of life. Each question requires a 1 – 5 rating response, indicating the degree of difficulty experienced. Here are some examples:

> DURING THE PAST WEEK, how much trouble did you have:
> Getting dressed? (physical)
> Taking a bath or shower? (physical)
> Walking? (physical)
> Speaking? (communication)
> Getting other people to understand you? (communication)
> Finding the word you wanted to say? (communication)
>
> DURING THE LAST WEEK did you:
> Feel discouraged about your future (psycho-social)
> Feel withdrawn from other people (psycho-social)
> See your friends less often than you would like (psycho-social)

Each question is rated 1 – 5, with 1 indicating 'Couldn't do at all'/ 'Definitely yes' and 5 indicating 'No trouble at all'/'Definitely no'.

The SAQOL-39 was adapted from a pre-existing stroke questionnaire. The changes aimed to make it accessible to people with aphasia (Hilari & Byng, 2001). For example, the wording of questions was simplified, and alterations were made to the layout, including font size and the number of questions per page. The measure has been extensively researched, with findings showing that people with mild or moderate aphasia can successfully complete the SAQOL-39 and that the data are reliable (Hilari et al, 2003). The latter means that if the measure is administered twice with the same person, over a limited period of time, the scores are very similar. This is important. It shows that the measure is stable, or that scores do not vary erratically. It also suggests that if there *is* a change in a person's score on the SAQOL-39 it reflects a genuine shift in their quality of life.

There are lots of benefits in using a questionnaire like the SAQOL-39. It is quick to administer and yields trustworthy results. It can track change over time, or in response to therapy. It can also be used to compare quality of life in different groups of people, such as stroke survivors who do and do not have aphasia. It has been translated into many different languages, so can be used with people whose first language is not English (e.g. Guo et al, 2016).

Of course, there are also limitations. You may worry about the depth of information that can be provided by questionnaire responses. For example, we can learn from the SAQOL-39 that a person had difficulty speaking in the last week, but not about the nature of that difficulty or how it felt. Such depth is more readily provided by other techniques, such as interviewing.

A number of studies have been conducted in which people with aphasia were interviewed about their experiences (e.g. Parr et al, 1997; Northcott & Hilari, 2011; Taubner et al, 2020). Many adaptations are made to enable people with aphasia to take part in this form of research. Questions are worded as simply as possible and often supported with gestures, drawing or written information. For those with little or no speech, closed format questions (requiring a yes/no response) are used. When evaluating responses to questions the researcher attends not just to what is said, but also to any non-verbal communication such as gesture and facial expression. Researchers frequently ask follow-up questions to check responses and ensure that they have fully understood what the person with aphasia wants to say. With adaptations such as these, interview studies have provided particularly rich information about how aphasia affects individuals' lives, how people cope, and what it feels like.

Interviews are not the only method of eliciting insights about aphasia. Researchers can also bring people together in focus groups. Led by a facilitator, such groups aim to discuss and seek common ground on key topics. In the context of aphasia, they have been used to explore the experiences of family members (Avent et al, 2005; Shafer et al, 2019) and views about different forms of intervention (e.g. Kincheloe et al, 2023). Researchers can also exploit relevant pre-existing sources. For example, Fotiadou and colleagues (2014) analysed online blogs produced by people with aphasia.

What about those with very severe aphasia? These individuals would struggle to complete questionnaires or take part in interviews, let alone write a blog. What can we do to capture their experiences? One method uses proxy respondents (Hilari & Byng, 2009). Here, someone who is very close to the person with aphasia completes a questionnaire on their behalf. While indicative, we cannot be sure that proxy responses accurately reflect the views of the person with aphasia. Indeed, there is some evidence that proxy responses are more negative than self-reports. In other words, when rating the quality of life of a relative, a proxy may score this lower than if the person rates themself (Cruice et al, 2005).

Another approach uses **ethnography**. This encompasses a range of methods such as observation, interaction, interviewing and analysis of artefacts. The approach was used by Susie Parr to explore the experiences of 20 people with severe aphasia (Parr, 2007). Each person was visited three times in a setting that reflected their day-to-day life. For example, Terry was observed at home alone, in respite care and at a day centre. The researcher recorded what happened in each setting, with accounts of the physical environment and verbatim instances of communication. On some occasions, she became involved in activities or con-tributed to conversations, particularly if participants were observed alone. Participants were also asked direct questions and carers were interviewed. Relevant artefacts included written materials, such as notices in the day centre and policy documents. These multiple sources of information were recorded in field notes, offering a detailed description of what was observed, and often allowing complex meanings to emerge. To illustrate, here is a brief clip from the appendix of the paper, in which Parr is recording observations of Terry at home:

> 'I remember the stark, dingy bedroom at Meerwood House (the respite care centre) and say: "Do you prefer to be at home?" He grimaces again: "Well" again with an uncertain intonation. He jumps up again, goes out and comes back with a spiral bound notebook and a biro. He writes: "JOPS." and says: "Better, this. It's all gone you see. All gone." "You want to work?" I venture. "That's it. That's it. But it's all gone." He points round the room to all the furniture, which his wife had told me he made before his stroke. "It's gone."
>
> (Parr, 2007, p 123)

This excerpt strongly conveys the changes in Terry's life and his sense of loss over those changes. It also shows how careful observation and enquiry enabled him to express his feelings, despite the limitations of his language.

Interview, focus group and ethnographic studies yield a daunting body of data, e.g. in form of transcripts and notes. Distilling these into clear findings is no simple task. Fortunately, there are recognised analytical techniques. For example, the Framework Method (Ritchie & Lewis, 2003) involves identifying common themes in the data and charting examples of each theme from the participants' records. These are then synthesised into a coherent narrative. In many studies, the analysed data are shared with the participants before publication, to ensure that they accurately reflect their views.

LIVING WITH APHASIA: KEY FINDINGS FROM RESEARCH

So, what have these methods revealed about the effects of aphasia on a person's life? Let's cover some general findings first.

Aphasia has a major impact on quality of life. When stroke survivors with and without aphasia are compared on quality of life questionnaires, those with aphasia score significantly worse; and this is the case even if their physical status, emotional wellbeing and social support mechanisms are comparable (Hilari, 2011). The degree of aphasia is also important. People with severe aphasia have lower quality of life scores than those with mild or moderate aphasia (Hilari & Byng, 2009).

Aphasia also threatens emotional wellbeing, with one study reporting that over 60% of people with aphasia had depression (Kauhanen et al, 2000). Christina Zanella and colleagues examined 970 patient records taken from a stroke care centre over one year (Zanella et al, 2023). They were interested in the incidence of post stroke depression and what influenced this. The findings couldn't have been clearer. The stroke patients with aphasia were seven times more likely to have depression than those without aphasia. The incidence of depression was not affected by age, gender or race. But it was affected by aphasia severity. As severity increased so too did the likelihood of depression.

People with aphasia take part in fewer social activities than their healthy peers (Cruice et al, 2006). They are also less active than stroke survivors without aphasia (Hilari, 2011). Aphasia is associated with reduced social networks, with friendships being particularly vulnerable (Hilari & Northcott, 2017). For example, in one study involving 83 people with aphasia, 64% reported that they saw their friends less often than before the stroke, and nearly a third retained no close friends (Hilari and Northcott, 2006).

PERSONAL ACCOUNTS

Interview and other qualitative data collected from people with aphasia add depth to these findings.

Feelings Associated with Aphasia

Those interviewed by Parr and colleagues (1997) reported feelings of fear, devastation, isolation and anger, particularly in the early days post stroke:

> *'Is frightened. Is frightened'*
>
> *(unattributed, p 10)*

> *'I Couldn't work out how I was going to carry on'*
>
> *(Christopher, p 15)*

> *'Oh my God. I want to die – when I could not speak – Because I know I could not live that way'*
>
> *(Govi, p 16)*

'I was mad. I was mad in here that it wouldn't come out – when I did try to say to something um … and it all come out … well gobbledegook … um … and I knew what I was going to say but I couldn't say it and I used to get mad – mad with myself'

(Pearl, p 15)

Social Losses

Numerous personal accounts describe how stroke and aphasia has taken away valued social roles, particularly relating to employment. Thirty-six of the people interviewed by Parr and colleagues (1997) were working prior to their stroke; but afterwards this reduced to five, and only one person retained their previous full-time job. For many, the loss of work was deeply felt, as voiced by Stephen:

'I love work. I love work and it's no good. – Eight years ago is on the telephone chat chat chat all day for me. And now is finished. – It's a blank. – My speech is just tongue-tied. Unbelievable is so awful'

(Parr et al, 1997; p 103)

Julie Morris and her fellow researchers (2011) describe the experiences of GD, who attempted to return to his job in an insurance company following stroke and aphasia. If you want to read more their paper is summarised in Box 6.1.

Social losses are not restricted to employment. Many of those interviewed by Parr et al (1997) described profound and in some cases painful shifts in their marriages, as partners had to become the principal earner or take on new caring responsibilities.

'My wife has been the carer all the way through. – I don't take no responsibility whatsoever now. In fact when I go out I don't even carry money. Because the wife does everything.'

(Les, p 47)

For some, new inequalities in their relationship, together with communication barriers, led to marital stresses. Rose's marriage was described as 'extremely close', but things were difficult in the early days following her stroke:

Box 6.1 Returning to work after stroke and aphasia: A case study (Morris et al, 2011)

GD was 45 when he had his stroke. He was living at home with his wife and two teenage children and worked for an insurance company as an accounts manager.

GD had mild aphasia. He had occasional word finding difficulties and problems understanding group and telephone conversations, particularly if there was background noise. He could still read complex documents, but often had to go back over sections. Writing was also slow. For example, it took him 3 or 4 hours to write a two page letter, and this would require editing. All GD's language problems were subtle, and not detected by standard aphasia assessments. He also performed normally on cognitive tests although GD felt that he had trouble remembering detailed information.

GD was keen to return to work. His rehabilitation was therefore entirely focussed on skills that he would need in his job. He received 36 hours of group and individual therapy working on employment related tasks. For example, he practised listening to and taking notes from work related phone messages. He composed emails from verbal instructions, and took minutes from recorded discussions. He practised writing and delivering presentations. He worked on memory strategies, such as keeping a diary and noting down key events in his day.

GD's ratings on a disability questionnaire improved as a result of this therapy and he felt ready to return to work. GD reported that his company was highly supportive. They encouraged him to keep in touch during his rehabilitation through occasional meetings and email updates. They agreed a return-to-work package, in which GD worked part time on a flexible basis. He was given a new role working from home managing a client data base. This involved less travel and less client contact than his pre-stroke job description.

Despite the careful preparation, GD's return to work was not sustained. After 19 months he was made redundant.

GD was interviewed about his experiences at work and to find out why the return broke down. Several factors emerged. From the outset, there was a lack of structure and he had very limited contact with his line manager. Most interactions with colleagues took place on the phone, which was difficult for GD. His new role did not play to his strengths, as he was not an IT expert. He had to attend regional meetings, which he found challenging owing to the number of people speaking and problems with background noise. He was also reluctant to contribute, owing to fears that he might stumble on his words. Most of GD's work mates were unaware of his stroke and aphasia, so did not make adjustments for him.

When the end came, GD was frustrated that his company did not consider further changes to his role, even if this meant a reduced salary.

The authors of the paper (who included GD) make additional points in their discussion. GD's role imposed high level language demands that were extremely challenging even for someone with mild aphasia. His speech and language therapist was keen to visit his work, to assess the demands of his job and discuss these with his manager. She also wanted to provide information about aphasia to GD's manager and workmates. However, GD did not permit this, preferring all communication with his workplace to come through him. He also tended to conceal his aphasia at work, saying instead that he had a problem with his hearing. Had GD been more open about his aphasia and allowed contact between his manager and the therapist, further adjustments might have been made.

GD's story demonstrates the complexities of returning to work for people with aphasia and the levels of support that this requires. Although GD was not able to resume his former work in the long term, the authors of the paper still insist that his is a success story. He progressed to a number of volunteering roles, particularly supporting other people with aphasia.

> 'He would go to work at eight and he'd come home at seven or eight and I was up with the children and go to bed with the children, so our relationship suffered of course … . He's very eloquent and very articulate and I mean no way could I top that because he was just so overpowering.. he'd sort of make me feel so inadequate and shitty'
>
> Rose; p 46.

Other family roles are also affected. Many individuals with aphasia describe instances in which they felt inadequate as a parent, for example because they could not answer their child's questions or support them during difficult transitions. Some report increased conflict with adolescent children. Laura, writing in a blog, describes the difficulties of reading to her child, while Fred was dismayed by his inability to speak at his daughter's wedding:

> 'Last week she (daughter) wanted me to read The Three Little Pigs, but it's hard to be convincing when the evil wolf sounds like this: me: 'Little Pig, Little Pig, let me out!' [daughter]: 'You mean, Let me in'.
>
> (Laura, quoted in Fotiadou et al, 2014; p 1289)

> *'It's things like my daughter's wedding. I couldn't speak. I had to write it all down and my brother-in-law done it all. Talked for me. Done it all for me.'*
> *(Fred, quoted in Parr et al, 1997; p 54)*

Some describe feeling overwhelmed by family gatherings and needing to withdraw. Painful family events, such as bereavements or a serious illness in a relative, can be particularly difficult for a person with aphasia.

Despite the pressures, family relationships typically survive stroke and aphasia. But, as we saw earlier, this is less true of friendships. Many personal accounts describe being abandoned by friends, in some cases rapidly following the stroke:

> *'Just gone. This is it. They gone … er … about six weeks gone.'*
> *(Susan, quoted in Parr et al, 1997; p 58)*

There seem to be several reasons behind friendship loss. Some are directly related to the aphasia, such as being unable to converse, or tell jokes and stories:

> *'I didn't feel that I had the right level of conversation to hold myself up in company … . I didn't feel that I could I suppose inflict myself. I didn't want to go to places and not be able to contribute in every way, I didn't feel I could.'*
> *(Patricia, quoted in Northcott & Hilari, 2011; p 531)*

Keeping up with the pace of talk can also be a problem:

> *'I used to talk very fast. – I have the humour still but I cannot talk fast enough'*
> *(Kiran, quoted in Parr et al, 1997, p 59)*

Difficulties with using the phone and with written communication can cause loss of contact with long-distance friends. Some people report negative reactions to their aphasia from friends, including being patronised, or even mocked:

> *'They laugh at me if it mistake … That's why sometimes I just keep quiet [crying]'*
> *(unattributed, quoted in Northcott & Hilari, 2011; p 528)*

Such negative responses seem a particular risk when the aphasia is severe, as recounted by one family member:

> *'One chap came, he did come a couple of times, but they seemed to sort of, they bossed Rog about and I hated that. Now come along, I'm sure you could say more than that, and I wanted to slap them quite honestly. I hated it when people told him what he could say and what he couldn't say, I felt as if he was being bullied'*
>
> *(Wendy, quoted in Parr, 2007; p 111)*

The wider consequences of stroke can also get in the way of friendships, such as problems travelling, loss of shared activities and fatigue. For some, stroke and aphasia lead to a shift in social desires, and feelings of withdrawal:

> *'I just don't feel like going out now ... just I seem to be closing in on myself'*
>
> *(Gordon, quoted in Northcott & Hilari, 2011; p 529)*

Personal Identity

We have seen how stroke and aphasia can run riot through a person's life, with losses of employment, shifts in family dynamics and abandoned friendships. Future plans often come to a shuddering halt, for example affecting the take up of educational and vocational opportunities, or the anticipated pleasures of retirement. Those with complex needs may have to leave their home and move into residential care, where little is known about their former life or personality. Such seismic changes are all the more difficult to negotiate when you cannot easily express your feelings or voice your preferences.

The losses associated with stroke and aphasia can undermine a person's sense of who they are, leading some to describe aphasia as 'identity theft' (Shadden, 2005). For example, Mike felt that he had lost his adulthood:

> *'I was bloody daft. Like a school kid'*
>
> *(Parr et al. 1997 p 13)*

While Tom described how aphasia had taken away a key part of himself:

> *'We have lost the use of words, and thereby a piece of ourselves. […] For someone who used words for 40 years, it completely changes my life.'*
> *(Fotiadou, 2014, p 1288)*

Helena Taubner and colleagues (2020) interviewed 9 people with aphasia about their post-stroke sense of identity. Only two of those interviewed felt that they were the same person as pre-stroke, and interestingly both had retained their former jobs. The others all expressed feelings of identity loss, in some cases with a sense of grief:

> *Interviewer: Are you the same person now as you were before the stroke?*
>
> *Oskar: No. […] Teach/tea/teacher, no, not now.*
>
> *(P 307)*
>
> *Ellen: You mourn, well, who you were, yourself.*
>
> *(p 309)*

Effects on Family Members

The effects of aphasia are not confined to stroke survivors. Their family members also report profound changes to their lives. Negative consequences experienced by some (but not all) relatives include increased stress, depression, loss of leisure and other activities, changes in work roles and marital difficulties (Grawberg et al, 2013a).

Many personal accounts from family members document the all-consuming nature of stroke and aphasia. New responsibilities can include physical care, mediating communication, organising services and supporting rehabilitation. Many feel that they have to advocate for their relative, and fight for provision. For some the burden of responsibility is extreme:

> *'After my husband's stroke, I felt a tremendous responsibility, as though I held Lewis's life in my hands'*
> *(Helen, quoted in Greenfield & Ganzfried, 2016)*

Others report how their own interests and concerns are subsumed. For example, Janice talks about the active and independent lives that she and her husband shared before his strokes, and how all balance was lost afterwards:

> *'Now we are at a place where both of us are living one life.. his'*
> *(quoted in Greenfield & Ganzfried, 2016)*

When asked about their needs, family members particularly highlight the importance of information (Avent et al, 2005). Many are initially baffled by their relative's aphasia and have multiple questions: Why can't he talk? Is he confused? Will he talk again? How can I help? Can he understand what I say? While wanting honest answers to these questions, relatives also flag the importance of hope. They find negative pronouncements, such as 'he will never talk again', particularly unhelpful.

Relatives may suffer from a lack of awareness in other people, as they observe their loved one being ignored, talked over or patronised. Some confront unhelpful myths, such as the assumption that they have supernatural powers of interpretation:

> *'With aphasia the caregiver is often placed in the role of translator. Even though I could sometimes spend twenty minutes trying to understand what Lewis wanted for lunch, people just naturally assumed that I understood everything that was on his mind.'*
> *(Helen, quoted in Greenfield & Ganzfried, 2016)*

Above all, personal accounts stress that adaptation to stroke and aphasia in a family member is a long-term process that changes over time. The early days post stroke may be consumed with fears for the relative's survival. As the person becomes medically stable, the family begins to confront the disabilities caused by the stroke and shift their focus to rehabilitation. Discharge from hospital is often a watershed, as the lasting impacts of the stroke become more evident and there are increased worries about how the family will cope. In the longer term, family roles and responsibilities are often completely re-configured. For those wishing to read more, Box 6.2 describes a daughter's adaptation to her father's aphasia in the year following his stroke.

Box 6.2 A case study of a daughter's adaptation to her father's aphasia and stroke (Le Dorze et al, 2009)

This paper focuses on the 31 year old daughter of a man with aphasia. For convenience, I will refer to her as 'X'. An only child, X was living at home with her parents at the time of her father's stroke. He was 60 years old and had severe aphasia.

X was interviewed three times. The first interview was four months after her father's stroke, at the start of his outpatient rehabilitation. The second was seven months post stroke, towards the end of rehabilitation and the last was three months later. The interviews covered three main themes relating to the stresses affecting X, the strategies that she was using to cope and her adaptation. X was asked about all stages of her father's stroke, including the very early days.

Initially, many of X's stresses related to her father's health and fears that he would die. Worries about his communication and the loss of their pre-stroke rapport became more prominent after his return home and as the permanence of his aphasia became clear.

> Uh ... and all the the conversation, you know sometimes, often we sat and I was, I knew that I couldn't uh, chat like before. This this was hard ... This, I'd say this was what was, what was, what was the most painful ... yeah. (p 492)

During the course of her father's rehabilitation X became concerned and often frustrated about the level of services available. She was angered by the speech and language therapist who said that her father would never talk again. She worried about her father's response to therapy and lack of progress. Later stresses also related to her own life. She had a long-term companion who she felt was not sufficiently supportive; and by the last interview this relationship had broken down.

A key strategy used by X at all stages of her father's recovery was to seek information about stroke and aphasia. She conducted extensive internet searches, joined online forums, used the hospital library and consulted his medical and rehabilitation team. Another important strategy was to advocate for services. For example, she argued for his speech and language therapy to be extended and engaged a private therapist. When her father returned home, she employed communication strategies, such as asking yes/no questions and using visual supports. She learnt to avoid conversation topics that distressed her parents, such as her father's health and recovery. She stressed the importance of staying hopeful. In the later interviews X was using strategies to improve her own situation, such as confiding in her aunts, taking more time for herself, and resuming her own leisure activities.

In the very early stages of her father's stroke, there were few indicators of adaptation. Rather X described the first weeks as *'absolute hell'*. The painful emotions persisted, as X mourned the loss of her pre-stroke father. However, she also began to take comfort in her strength and ability to fight on his behalf. In the final interview, she described learning to live with her father's stroke and aphasia, but still found it very difficult to accept:

You learn to live with it, for sure, it diminishes, you find ways to deal with it uh. You re- ... Everything changes, every, every, every life of people around changes uh. That's about adaptation and ... But to go as far as to accept, accept, that. No. (p 495)

LIVING WELL WITH APHASIA

This chapter has highlighted the losses associated with stroke and aphasia, both for those affected and their family members. You may be wondering if these losses are inevitable, or even if there are any gains.

Some of the individuals I worked with identified positive changes induced by their stroke. For example, relinquishing a stressful job with punishing working hours may be seen as a bonus, together with increased leisure time and a slower pace of life. Others point to new experiences gained through their stroke. One man set up a self-help group for people with aphasia in his local area, while another became highly involved in aphasia research, with new connections across several university departments. Changes in hobbies and interests, imposed by aphasia, may introduce the person to new activities that they would not have considered before their stroke, such as singing in a choir or painting. Many also enjoy new friendships within the aphasia community, brought about through membership of aphasia groups.

Involvement in religion is particularly important for some stoke survivors and I have met some who state that their faith was enhanced by their stroke. Laures-Gore and her fellow researchers interviewed 13 people about the role of spirituality in their aphasia recovery (Laures-Gore et al, 2018). Eleven of those interviewed felt that spirituality had played a part and nearly half spoke of God watching over them or being their active helper.

Grawberg et al (2013b) interviewed 20 relatives of people with aphasia, and included a specific question about any positive experiences. The reported gains related to emotions, communication, relationships, leisure activities, work and education. For example, relatives reported feelings of pride in their family member and an enhanced sense of closeness induced by the aphasia. Ironically, some felt that communication had improved with their relative since the stroke, e.g. because they were speaking more often and more openly. Some respondents had made new friends and taken up new activities because of their family member's stroke. There were examples of relatives gaining new knowledge about aphasia, with some changing direction in their career as a result of their experiences.

Although encouraging, accounts of positive experiences are far from universal and are typically outweighed by the negatives. What, therefore, determines whether an individual is able to re-build life after stroke and live well with aphasia? Brooke Grohn and her fellow researchers were interested to hear the views of people with aphasia on this question (Grohn et al, 2014). They interviewed 12 stroke survivors four times in the year following their stroke. During these meetings each person was asked to rate themselves as to whether or not they were living successfully with aphasia, using a scale ranging from 1 (for *not at all successful*) to 9 (for *very successful*). Their rating was then discussed with questions such as 'Why have you rated yourself at that point?', 'What would help you live more successfully?' and 'What has stopped you from living successfully?'

At one year post stroke most of the participants rated themselves above 5 on the scale, indicating that they were 'successful' or 'somewhat successful' in living with aphasia. In discussion, four main themes emerged as being associated with success. The first was the perception of improvement, particularly in communication skills. This did not have to mean full recovery, but there did need to be a sense of progression. For example, one of the interviewees took delight in being able to write to her grandchild for the first time since her stroke. The second theme was being involved in meaningful activities. Although some activities were lost, for example relating to employment, interviewees valued those that remained, such as trips with family and friends, attending sports events and even housework. Community activities, such as volunteering, were also cited, in some cases as a future ambition. The third theme was the availability of support, particularly from family members but also through rehabilitation services; and the final theme was maintaining positivity, which for some included battling with negative emotions. The authors suggest that these four themes contribute to an overarching theme of 'actively moving forward'.

MAINTAINING COMMUNICATION

We have heard how people with aphasia often experience social exclusion and communication barriers with family and friends. However, this is not always the case. We also see numerous instances where communication is sustained despite the aphasia. This is particularly facilitated if family members or friends are informed about aphasia and able to adapt their communication.

To illustrate, let's return to Rachel.

Simone was a long-standing friend of Rachel's, who shared her interest in history of art. After Rachel's stroke she took an active role in Rachel's care. She supported her move into a residential home and helped to manage her finances. She also kept up the friendship, for example, by visiting regularly and taking Rachel on trips.

Watching Simone and Rachel in conversation was a delight. You will remember that Rachel's speech consisted almost entirely of incomprehensible jargon, with virtually no real words. How, therefore, could she chat to Simone?

Simone set up her conversations with Rachel carefully. She would sit near her and make sure there were no distractions, e.g., by turning off the TV. She usually brought along useful visual props. For example, if she was telling Rachel about an exhibition, she would bring the catalogue. She spoke slightly more slowly than usual, without being abnormally slow or patronising. Above all, she had excellent strategies for coping with Rachel's jargon. She avoided asking questions that Rachel could not answer, such as 'who painted this?' Instead, she often invited Rachel to express her feelings, as these could usually be interpreted from her tone of voice. When Rachel was speaking, she did not pretend that she understood her jargon. On the other hand, she did not ask her to correct it, as she knew Rachel could not do this. She was very sensitive to Rachel's non-verbal communication, such as her facial expressions and intonation, and often responded to this. She was careful to preserve Rachel's dignity and continued to respect her academic knowledge. A particular instance illustrates these skills. Simone was showing Rachel the catalogue of an art exhibition that she had visited. She pointed to reproductions of the pictures that she saw and made observations about their subject matter. At one point she asked Rachel if she was familiar with one of the paintings. When Rachel nodded 'yes' she asked 'What do you think of it?' Rachel then embarked on a long discourse in jargon. Although the content could not be understood, her tone of voice was enthusiastic, and her speech was accompanied by emphatic hand gestures. Simone listened calmly and smiled. When Rachel paused, she said: 'It sounds like you are very keen on this work', which Rachel confirmed. She then asked if Rachel had studied or written about the artist. Rachel indicated that she had not but pulled out a book from her shelves. She led Simone to a chapter about an artist from a similar period.

SUMMARY AND TAKE HOME MESSAGES

A range of research techniques has enabled stroke survivors to tell us about how aphasia has affected their lives.

The findings indicate that quality of life is severely impacted. Stroke survivors with aphasia have lower quality of life scores than those without, and people with severe aphasia fare worst of all. This shows that language loss has detrimental effects that are over and above other stroke impairments.

Emotional well-being also takes a hit, and the risk of depression is particularly high in people with aphasia.

Personal accounts document many social losses arising from stroke and aphasia, for example affecting employment, family roles and friendships. The combined effects can leave the person feeling that they are no longer the same person that they were before their stroke.

The lives of family members are also changed when a relative has a stroke and aphasia. Many family members have to reconfigure their work and social lives in order to fulfil caring responsibilities, and family relationships can fall under stress.

Although many of the impacts of stroke and aphasia are negative, some positive findings have also been reported. For example, some family members feel closer to their relative post stroke, while others value the insights and new experiences gained through their encounter with aphasia. Some individuals report living successfully with aphasia. Factors that make this possible include a feeling of progression in rehabilitation, involvement in meaningful activities, the availability of support and maintaining a positive outlook.

The chapter ended by illustrating how communication can proceed, even in the face of severe aphasia. Despite her jargon, Rachel's conversation with Simone enabled her to express her passion for art and validated her identity as a respected art historian.

Maintaining communication, improving quality of life and enabling the person to live well despite their language impairments are key goals in aphasia therapy. Recovery and rehabilitation are the topics of our final chapter.

REFERENCES

Avent, J., Glista, S., Wallace, S., Jackson, J., Nishioka, J., & Yip, W. (2005). Family information needs about aphasia. *Aphasiology*, 19, 365–375. 10.1080/02687030444000813

Cruice, M., Worrall, L., Hickson, L. and Murison, R. (2005) Measuring quality of life: Comparing family members' and friends' ratings with those of their aphasic partners. *Aphasiology*, 19, 111–129. DOI: 10.1080/02687030444000651

Cruice, M., Worrall, L., & Hickson, L. (2006). Quantifying aphasic people's social lives in the context of non-aphasic peers. *Aphasiology*, 20, 12, 1210–1225. 10.1080/02687030600790136

Fotiadou, D., Northcott, S., Chatzidaki, A. & Hilari, K. (2014) Aphasia blog talk: How does stroke and aphasia affect a person's social relationships? *Aphasiology*, 28, 11, 1281–1300, DOI: 10.1080/02687038.2014.928664

Greenfield, E. & Ganzfried, M. (2016) *The Word Escapes Me: Voices of Aphasia*. Balboa Press

Grawburg, M., Howe, T., Worrall, L., & Scarinci, N. (2013a). Third-party disability in family members of people with aphasia: A systematic review. *Disability and Rehabilitation*, 35(16), 1324–1341. 10.3109/09638288.2012.735341

Grawburg, M., Howe, T., Worrall, L. & Scarinci, N. (2013b) A qualitative investigation into third-party functioning and third-party disability in aphasia: Positive and negative experiences of family members of people with aphasia, *Aphasiology*, 27:7, 828–848, DOI: 10.1080/02687038.2013.768330

Grohn, B., Worrall, L., Simmons-Mackie, N. & Hudson, K. (2014) Living successfully with aphasia during the first year post-stroke: A longitudinal qualitative study, *Aphasiology*, 28, 12, 1405–1425, DOI: 10.1080/02687038. 2014.935118

Guo, Y. E., Togher, L., Power, E., & Koh, G. C. H. (2016). Validation of the stroke and aphasia quality of life scale in a multicultural population. *Disability and Rehabilitation*, 38(26), 2584–2592. 10.3109/09638288.2016.1138551

Hilari, K. (2011). The impact of stroke: Are people with aphasia different to those without? *Disability and Rehabilitation*, 33(3), 211–218. 10.3109/09638288.2010. 508829

Hilari, K., & Byng, S. (2001). Measuring quality of life in people with aphasia: The stroke specific quality of life scale. *International Journal of Language & Communication Disorders*, 36(S1), 86–91. 10.3109/13682820109177864

Hilari, K., Byng, S., Lampling, D. L., & Smith, S. C. (2003). Stroke and aphasia quality of life scale-39 (SAQOL-39): Evaluation of acceptability, reliability, and validity. *Stroke*, 34, 8, 1944–1950. 10.1161/01.STR.0000081987.46660.ED

Hilari, K. and Nothcott, S., (2006), Social support in people with chronic aphasia. *Aphasiology*, 20, 1, 17–36. 10.1080/02687030500279982

Hilari, K., & Byng, S. (2009). Health-related quality of life in people with severe aphasia. *International Journal of Language & Communication Disorders*, 44(2), 193–205. 10.1080/13682820802008820

Hilari, K., & Northcott, S. (2017). "Struggling to stay connected": Comparing the social relationships of healthy older people and people with stroke and aphasia. *Aphasiology*, 31(6), 674–687. 10.1080/02687038.2016.1218436

Kauhanen, M.L., Korpelainen, J.T., Hiltunen, P., Määttä, R., Mononen, H., Brusin, E., Sotaniemi, K.A., & Myllylä, V.V. (2000) Aphasia, depression, and non-verbal cognitive impairment in ischaemic stroke. *Cerebrovascular Diorders* 10(6), 455–461. doi: 10.1159/000016107. PMID: 11070376.

Kincheloe, H., Off, C., Murphy, M., Griffin-Musick, J., Murray, K., & Jakober, D. (2023). "We all have coping and communication problems". Experiences of stroke survivors living with aphasia and graduate student clinicians who participated in a telehealth interprofessional psychoeducation and wellness group. *Aphasiology*, 37, 3, 408–431. 10.1080/02687038.2021.2020716

Laures-Gore, J. S., Lambert, P. L., Kruger, A. C., Love, J., & Davis, D. E. (2018). Spirituality and post-stroke aphasia recovery. *Journal of Religion and Health*, 57(5), 1876–1888. 10.1007/s10943-018-0592-4

Le Dorze, G., Tremblay, V. & Croteau, C. (2009) A qualitative longitudinal case study of a daughter's adaptation process to her father's aphasia and stroke. *Aphasiology*, 23, 4, 483–502, DOI: 10.1080/02687030801890909

Morris, J., Franklin, S., Menger, F., & GD. (2011). Returning to work with aphasia: A case study. *Aphasiology*, 25(8), 890–907. 10.1080/02687038.2010. 549568

Northcott, S., & Hilari, K. (2011). Why do people lose their friends after a stroke? *International Journal of Language & Communication Disorders*, 46(5), 524–534. 10.1111/j.1460-6984.2011.00079.x

Parr, S. (2007). Living with severe aphasia: Tracking social exclusion. *Aphasiology*, 21(1), 98–123. 10.1080/02687030600798337

Parr, S., Byng, S., & Gilpin, S. (1997) *Talking about Aphasia*. Buckingham: Open University Press.

Ritchie, J., & Lewis, J. (2003). *Qualitative Research Practice—A Guide for Social Science Students and Researchers*. London, Thousand Oaks, CA: Sage Publications Ltd.

Shadden, B. B. (2005). Aphasia as identify theft: Theory and practice. *Aphasiology*, 19, 3–5, 211–223. 10.1080/02687930444000697

Shafer, J. S., Shafer, P. R., & Haley, K. L. (2019). Caregivers navigating rehabilitative care for people with aphasia after stroke: A multi-lens perspective. *International Journal of Language & Communication Disorders*, 54, 4, 634–644. 10.1111/1460-6984.12467

Taubner, H., Hallén, M., Wengelin, Å., (2020). Still the same? Self-identity dilemmas when living with post-stroke aphasia in a digitalised society. *Aphasiology*, 34, 3, 300–318. 10.1080/02687038.2019.1594151

Zanella, C., Laures-Gore, J., Dotson, V.M., & Belagaje, S.R. (2023) Incidence of post-stroke depression symptoms and potential risk factors in adults with aphasia in a comprehensive stroke center. *Topics in Stroke Rehabilitation*, 30(5), 448–458. doi: 10.1080/10749357.2022.2070363. Epub 2022 May 11. PMID: 35543182; PMCID: PMC9649834.

7

WILL HE GET BETTER? RECOVERY AND REHABILITATION

Let's start with the good news. Most stroke survivors with aphasia experience some degree of recovery, both spontaneously and in response to therapy. Improvement is most rapid and marked in the early days post stroke. But changes can occur even many years later, particularly as a result of therapy. Change can take many forms. There may be improvements in the processing of language, for example affecting the production and comprehension of words. Individuals can also become more effective communicators despite their aphasia, for example because they are making effective use of strategies. Training family members and friends, so that they better understand aphasia and have skills for supporting communication, can improve communication in the home; and approaches have been developed that address the social and emotional consequences of aphasia. On the downside, aphasia rarely resolves completely, particularly if it is severe. Treatments are therefore looking to reduce and mitigate the problems, rather than bring about a cure.

This chapter will first discuss recovery in aphasia and factors that affect this. It will then briefly describe how aphasia rehabilitation is organised, before focusing on specific treatment approaches. I will use the now familiar boxes to describe exemplary therapy studies. These also illustrate how treatment outcomes are researched, or how we know whether or not our therapies work.

RECOVERY

Strokes have many detrimental effects on the brain. There is a core area of damage, often called the **lesion** site, where cells are

DOI: 10.4324/9781003382737-7

destroyed by the interruption of blood supply. Blood flow is also typically reduced in the area surrounding this site, with the risk of further cell damage. Brain regions that are connected to, but remote from the lesion can suffer because they are no longer receiving input from the damaged area; and swelling can affect multiple regions both on the surface and deep within the brain.

In the period immediately following the stroke some of these detrimental effects resolve, resulting in spontaneous recovery. For example, the swelling reduces and blood flow may improve to areas beyond the lesion. Some (but not all) individuals can benefit from **thrombolysis**. This is a medical intervention that aims to dissolve the blood clot that caused the stroke and restore blood supply to the surviving brain tissue. If provided within hours of the stroke this treatment can significantly improve outcomes. Surgery may also be used, for example to clear a blocked artery.

A key mechanism of recovery is **brain plasticity**, or the generation of new connections between areas of the brain unaffected by the stroke (e.g., Cramer, 2008). In effect, this redistributes responsibilities, with surviving brain regions assuming the roles of the damaged area. In the case of left hemisphere strokes causing aphasia, new connections may increase activation in the right hemisphere. However, the role of this activation in recovery is unclear. Saur and colleagues tracked the recovery of 14 people with aphasia in the year following their stroke (Saur et al., 2006). Each person was assessed repeatedly on a number of language assessments, and all showed significant improvements (they were receiving therapy for their aphasia). They were also scanned on three occasions using functional MRI. These scans recorded their brain activation while they carried out a language task (they listened to spoken sentences and judged whether or not they made sense). Early scans suggested that language improvements were associated with increased right hemisphere activation. However, by the third scan, when most recovery had taken place, the right hemisphere activation was reduced and replaced with greater activity in the left. The authors argue that there may be different stages of aphasia recovery. Initial gains may be supported by right hemisphere involvement. However, intact regions of the left hemisphere play a greater role in later stages, particularly for those with milder strokes who retain more viable left hemisphere tissue.

A number of factors affect recovery from stroke and aphasia (see Kiran and Thompson 2019 for a review of this topic). Some relate to the nature of the brain damage. Unsurprisingly, larger strokes are associated with poorer recovery, probably because there is less intact brain tissue on which to base the re-organisation of function. Research suggests that the location of the stroke is also important, with preservation of some left hemisphere regions being crucial for recovery. However, identifying these regions is problematic, as different studies have highlighted different areas.

A recent review of therapy outcome data from over 900 individuals with aphasia identified two predictors of recovery (Release, 2021). One was age, with younger stroke survivors doing best. This may be because youth is associated with brain plasticity; i.e., young brains may be more able to form new connections after damage than older brains. Indeed, children who survive strokes and have aphasia often demonstrate marked improvement which is associated with re-distributed patterns of activation across both hemispheres (Kojima et al., 2011). However, brain plasticity may not be the only reason. For example, younger stroke survivors may have better general health and more energy than their older counterparts, making them more able to profit from rehabilitation. And there is an important proviso about age. Although best outcomes were achieved by the younger Release group (<55 years old) all age groups demonstrated gains, even those over 75. The data do not, therefore, argue for the exclusion of older people from therapy.

The other factor identified by the Release data was the timing of therapy. Those who received therapy soon after the stroke did better than those who were treated later. This is probably because early therapy coincides with the period in which most spontaneous recovery is taking place. Importantly, all therapy administrations brought about improvements, even when provided more than six months post stroke. Therefore, if early therapy is not possible, for example because the person is not well, later rehabilitation is still potentially valuable.

Timing of therapy is not the only relevant variable. The amount of therapy received is also crucial, with best outcomes being associated with a high number of sessions delivered intensively (Brady et al., 2016; Brady et al., 2021). However, again the story is not straight forward. For example, the dropout rates from intensive therapy are high, and some people make good progress from more leisurely therapy regimes, with just two or three sessions per week.

To summarise so far, most people who have aphasia following a stroke will show at least some recovery. Some improvement is due to the spontaneous remission of stroke symptoms, but a major engine of change is rehabilitation. Those who receive a lot of therapy, ideally soon after their stroke, do best, but smaller amounts of therapy can be beneficial even years post stroke; and while youth is associated with better outcomes, gains are observed across all age groups.

TREATMENT DELIVERY

In the UK, stroke care for most patients begins with hospital admission, ideally as soon as possible after the stroke. This allows for emergency medical treatment, such as thrombolysis described above. As the person becomes medically stable, rehabilitation can begin. Depending on the effects of the stroke, the person should be supported by a multi-disciplinary team. Physical disabilities, for example affecting walking, are addressed by the physio therapists. Occupational therapists help the person with activities of daily living, such as washing, dressing and cooking, and advise on aids and adaptations in the home. Problems with language and communication are picked up by the speech and language therapists (SLTs). They therefore take the lead in aphasia rehabilitation. The SLTs also support those who have difficulties with eating and drinking. This may seem odd, but came about because of their expertise in the workings of the mouth and throat.

Those with persistent stroke disabilities should continue to receive rehabilitation after discharge from hospital. This may be provided in the person's own home, in the form of domiciliary therapy, or involve outpatient appointments in a hospital or other clinical setting. Some individuals are referred on to a residential rehabilitation centre, where they receive intensive input from a team of therapists. There is no standard duration of rehabilitation. Some receive therapy for months, while for others treatment is restricted to a few weeks.

Long-term support also varies. In some contexts, there is continuing NHS provision. For example, the person may be invited for reviews by the rehabilitation team and offered periods of "top up" therapy. Several voluntary organisations and charities provide services for stroke survivors, for example in the form of support groups or volunteer visiting schemes. Some universities that train speech and language therapists run aphasia clinics. These provide their students with clinical experience and offer additional therapy for local people living with aphasia. More affluent stroke survivors, or those with health insurance, may access private therapy.

By now, you will have gathered that there is no single model of stroke rehabilitation. Even within the UK, individuals have widely differing experiences, depending on their personal circumstances and local NHS practices. There are clinical guidelines for stroke services. For example, the UK National Institute for Health and Care Excellence (NICE) currently recommends that adults receiving stroke rehabilitation are offered at least 45 minutes of each relevant therapy for a minimum of five days a week. However, personal accounts and surveys of stroke survivors suggest that they often receive less than this, leading to concerns about health inequalities. Of course, such concerns magnify if we adopt an international perspective, with huge discrepancies across countries, depending on economic factors and the relative development of stroke services.

So far, I have discussed the timing and delivery of aphasia therapy, but not therapy content. I imagine that many readers will be wondering what such therapy involves. In fact, aphasia therapy encompasses a whole range of approaches, that aim to reduce the language impairment, develop communication skills, and improve quality of life. These therapies can be administered one-to-one or in groups. Therapy can work just with the aphasic person or involve those in their environment, such as family members. We can also engage technology, for example to enhance practice or to compensate for aphasic difficulties. The following sections describe examples of these different types of therapy.

IMPROVING LANGUAGE

Many treatments aim to improve language skills and hence reduce the symptoms of aphasia. There are numerous examples covering just about every aspect of language, including the production and comprehension of words, sentence construction, reading and writing. I will illustrate by focusing on therapy for word finding.

Almost everyone with aphasia experiences word finding problems. They report knowing what they want to say but being unable to think of the words that they need. The problem varies in severity. Some individuals are deprived of almost all their vocabulary, while others get stuck only on unusual words.

Treatments for word finding problems usually involve repetitive exercises with a target set of words. These exercises typically require the person to think about the meaning of the word and/or how it sounds. In most approaches the person is also asked to say the target word, for example by naming a picture. The therapies aim to stimulate access to words, so making them permanently more available.

A widely used word finding therapy is called Semantic Feature Analysis (Boyle, 2010). As the name implies this therapy aims to cue production by focussing on word meaning, or semantics. Here each word is practised using the following chart:

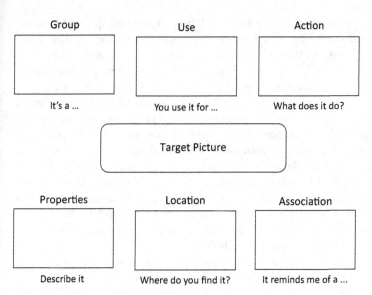

Figure 7.1 Semantic Feature Analysis Chart

Table 7.1 Questions that may be used in Semantic Feature Analysis (target: Cherry)

Box	Question	Possible Answers
GROUP	What type of thing is it?	Fruit
USE	What is it used for?	We eat it
ACTION	What does it do?	It grows on trees
PROPERTIES	What does it look like? What does it taste like?	It's red, shiny, small, round, sweet
LOCATION	Where do you find it?	In the fruit bowl; on a tree; in the garden; in an orchard; in the supermarket
ASSOCIATION	What does it make you think of?	Summer; the countryside

First of all, the therapist places a picture of the target word in the central box and asks the person to name it. Then the therapist asks a series of questions about the word, using each of the surrounding boxes. Let's imagine that the word is "cherry". Table 7.1 gives examples of possible questions and answers:

The answers are written in each box, so building up a profile of the word's meaning. If the person with aphasia struggles to answer the questions, the therapist can offer cues, such as forced alternatives ("is it yellow or red?"), yes/no prompts ("Do you drink it?") or encouragements to answer the question non-verbally ("Show me what you would do with it/where you would keep it"). Once all the questions have been answered the therapist asks the person to name the picture again. If they cannot, the therapist says the word for the person to repeat. The therapist then moves onto the next word, repeating all the steps. The number of words practiced using semantic Feature Analysis varies. People with severe aphasia may target just a few words, say 15, while those with milder problems can work with a larger set, such as 50. It is important to choose words that are relevant to the person's life. For example, they may relate to their practical needs or connect with a particular interest or hobby.

Semantic Feature Analysis has been quite extensively researched, so we know it can work. In this research, improvements are typically measured by using picture naming tests, administered before and after therapy. These tests include both practised and unpractised words. So, pursuing our example, the naming test will include "cherry", which has been practised, and possibly "peach", which has not. In most studies of Semantic Feature Analysis naming of the practised words improves after therapy. In some (but not all) studies unpractised words also improve, pointing to more wide-spread gains in word retrieval.

Box 7.1 describes a study of Semantic Feature Analysis. Here, the therapy was augmented with an additional task, in which the practised word had to be used in a phrase. This study also used a range of measures, to explore the possible wider benefits of therapy beyond word retrieval.

Box 7.1 A Randomised Controlled Study of Elaborated Semantic Features Analysis (Efstratiadou et al., 2019)

This Greek study involved 39 participants who had aphasia following a stroke. Their mean age was 58 (range 38–84) and their time post stroke ranged from 4–207 months. Participants had varying types and severities of aphasia although most were classed as moderately or severely impaired.

The research evaluated an Elaborated form of Semantic Feature Analysis (ESFA). Participants received 36 hours of therapy over 12 weeks, during which they practised a set of words, using a Greek version of the SFA chart described above. The elaboration required them also to produce the words in phrases, such as "cherries are red", "cherries are sweet" (of course they produced Greek equivalents). Participants either received individual therapy or a combination therapy, comprising two individual sessions and one group session per week. Group therapy sessions followed the same SFA procedures, but participants supported each other by, for example, suggesting features of the words or offering cues.

The study employed a rather complicated **randomised controlled design**. Eighteen participants were assigned to receive individual therapy, nine were assigned to receive combination therapy, and 12 were assigned to the control group. Each person was assessed four or five times on a range of measures (described below). The assessments took place when they first joined the study (week 1) and again six weeks later. No one had received therapy at this point, so these were both baseline assessments. The third assessment happened in week 19. This was after therapy for those in the individual and combined treatment groups. Those in the control group had still not received any therapy at this point, so it was their third baseline. After this assessment, the control participants were re-randomised either to receive individual or combined therapy. The previously treated participants received no further therapy. There was a fourth assessment at week 32. This was a post therapy assessment for the controls, and a follow-up assessment for the others. There was a fifth, follow up assessment just for the controls in week 45.

By now, your head may be reeling! So let me pull out the important features of the design. The multiple assessment points meant that everyone was assessed at least twice before they received therapy. They were assessed again immediately after therapy when any therapy gains should become evident. The follow up assessments, about 13 weeks later, explored whether those gains were maintained. This is important, as we want treatment effects to be durable and not fade away. The third assessment point, at week 19, was particularly telling. At this point the researchers can compare those who have been treated with the controls, who were yet to receive therapy. A positive effect of therapy is demonstrated here if the treated groups have improved significantly more than the controls.

Evaluation studies of therapy often use **primary and secondary outcome measures**. The primary measure is most expected to change because it is highly related to the content of therapy. The secondary measures explore possible treatment effects, so may also change, but equally may not. In this study the primary outcome measure was a 260-item picture naming test. A subset of these words was practised in therapy, so the researchers were hypothesising that scores on this test would improve. Naming of unpractised words was also tested in a secondary measure. Other secondary measures included an assessment of discourse, in which the person described a complex picture, a quality-of-life questionnaire, an assessment of mood, and a questionnaire about everyday communication, which was completed by a relative or friend of each participant. The assessments were administered by researchers who were **blinded** to group allocation. This means that they did not know whether the person being tested was assigned to a treatment or control group and is an important way of reducing **bias** in a study.

So, what happened? Let's take the primary outcome measure first. As predicted, this improved following therapy. The gains were also durable, so were still evident at follow up. Progress on this measure was clearly related to therapy. So, at week 19 the treated participants had improved significantly more than the controls. Encouragingly, the secondary naming measure also improved, suggesting that there were general gains in word finding that were not confined to practised words. Most other secondary measures were unchanged, although there was some positive movement on the quality of life and communication questionnaires. There were no differences in outcomes between those who received individual and combination therapy.

This study offers good evidence that ESFA can improve word finding in aphasia, as assessed by picture naming tests. There may be associated benefits for quality of life and everyday communication, although these need confirming in future research. The authors thought that those receiving combination therapy might do better on the measures of communication, as their therapy involved more social interaction. However, this was not the case. They suggest that more conversation practice in therapy might have enhanced their gains.

DEVELOPING COMMUNICATION SKILLS

If you ask people with aphasia what they want from therapy they flag many things, but high up the list is better communication (Worral et al., 2011). They want to converse, get their opinions across, tell stories and jokes. Those with severe problems want to overcome the many breakdowns in communication that dog their daily lives.

Improving everyday communication is one of the holy grails of aphasia therapy. We can try to achieve this by reducing the language impairment. However, as we saw in the previous section, language gains do not always translate into better communication. Rather, if you want to improve communication, the therapy needs to address this head on. In other words, the therapy itself needs to be communicative.

How is this done? In many instances, work on language skills is interwoven with tasks in which those skills are employed for communication. So, word finding treatments, such as Semantic Feature Analysis, may be followed by tasks in which the practised words are used to convey a message, or integrated into a conversation.

To illustrate this approach let's return to Rachel. You will remember that Rachel had Wernicke's aphasia with largely incomprehensible jargon speech. She also showed poor awareness of her difficulties. For example, she never expressed frustration over her speech or tried to correct it. Rachel was not well disposed towards speech and language therapy, given that she could not see the need for it. Previous attempts to work on her speech or encourage the use of communication strategies had been met with a raspberry.

In Chapter 4, I described investigations of Rachel's writing. Although her writing was severely impaired, here there were some hopeful signs. When attempting to write the names of pictures Rachel got some letters correct; and occasionally she could write the whole word if she was cued with the first letter. She could copy words, even if they were long, and even after an imposed delay. Above all, Rachel was aware of her writing problems and was willing to work on writing. From this, we developed a therapy plan. We aimed to build upon Rachel's writing skills and encourage her to use writing in her everyday communication. In consultation with Rachel's friends, we drew up lists of relevant words. These related to Rachel's daily needs, her leisure activities, and her academic interests. Rachel first practised writing these words, using a range of spelling activities. We then integrated the words into communication tasks. Therapy also included discussion with Rachel about how she might use her written words, for example when communicating with her carers. Those carers and her friends were advised to offer Rachel a pen and paper when they were communicating with her and to prompt her to write when communication broke down. We evaluated this therapy in a **single case experimental study**. The results showed that Rachel learnt how to write many of her practised words. In later therapy stages she used these words to answer conversational questions or convey a given message. By the end of therapy there were also occasions when Rachel used her writing in everyday communication. If you want to read more, Box 7.2 describes the study and tells you more about the therapy.

So far, I have described therapies that aim to build upon formal language skills, such as spoken and written word production. When aphasia is very severe achieving progress with these skills may be extremely difficult. Here, therapy may aim to exploit non-verbal strategies, such as gesture.

The potential of gesture to enhance communication in aphasia is beautifully illustrated in the following quote. This is an excerpt from

Box 7.2 A single case study of communication therapy using writing (Robson et al., 1998)

This paper describes three programmes of therapy that aimed to improve communication through the strategic use of writing. The study involved Rachel who had severe Wernicke's aphasia with incomprehensible jargon speech.

Before the first programme of therapy, we drew up a list of 74 words. These were discussed with Rachel's friends to ensure that they were relevant to her life. For example, they included words related to her home (RADIO, TELEVISION), food (SANDWICH, SOUP), holidays (TICKET, PASSPORT), visits (MUSEUM, GALLERY), and her academic specialism of Chinese ceramics (DRAGON, PHOENIX). The words were divided into two sets of 37 items. One set was practised in therapy. The other was unpractised, so acted as a control.

The first therapy programme consisted of 14 sessions. As in all the programmes, sessions lasted about 45 minutes and were scheduled two or three times per week. The therapy aimed to improve Rachel's spelling of the 37 target words using tasks that became progressively more difficult. In initial tasks she had to make judgements about the words; e.g., she was shown a picture of a television and given two Scrabble tiles (T and R) from which she had to pick the correct first letter. She then progressed to anagram tasks. Here she was given all the letters for a word and had to sort them into the correct order. Finally, she had to try writing the word. If she got stuck, the therapist cued her e.g., by providing the first letter. With the anagram and writing tasks Rachel was asked to judge whether her attempts were correct and, if not, try to put them right.

Therapy was evaluated by asking Rachel to write all 74 words before and after therapy. Before therapy she could write none of the words without help, whereas after therapy 14 were correct. There were also many instances where she could write part of the word, and often enough to make it guessable. Almost all her successes were in the practised set, showing that therapy was responsible for the improvement. The 37 treated words were tested again six weeks after therapy stopped. Rachel could still write six of the words without help and a further seven following a first letter cue.

The first programme showed that Rachel could improve her writing, albeit with a small number of words. She also enjoyed working on writing and was determined to continue. On the other hand, communication with Rachel was still very difficult and she was making no attempt to use her writing in her daily interactions.

A second programme of 15 sessions aimed to improve Rachel's spelling of more words and encourage the communicative use of writing. Eighteen words from the previous control set were practised using the spelling tasks described above. Eighteen words from the previously treated set were practised in communication tasks, in which Rachel had to use her words to convey a message. For example, in one task Rachel had to use writing to communicate the content of a hidden picture to a friend, in another she had to write down items that she would take on holiday and in a third she had to describe a day out. All of these tasks could be completed by using one or more of her practised words.

Rachel's writing improved further following this therapy. As in the first programme, Rachel was assessed before and after therapy on a written picture naming assessment. None of the words in the new treatment set were written correctly before therapy, whereas after therapy 15 (83%) were correct. A control set of 18 unpractised words showed no change. Rachel was also assessed before and after therapy on a conversation task. She was asked 36 questions, each of which could be answered with a treated word (e.g., "where would you go to see some paintings?" for GALLERY). Before therapy she wrote just four correct answers to these questions, after therapy, she wrote 21.

The second programme showed that Rachel could learn more written words and use those words to answer conversational questions. Yet, Rachel's friends observed that she was still not using writing in everyday communication. We therefore administered a third programme of therapy. This aimed to expand her written vocabulary by using the spelling tasks with new words, and further promote the communicative use of writing. It included a message task. Here, Rachel was given a written message, such as "My blouse has not come back from the laundry". She was then given two pictures of practised words (e.g., of a radio and a shirt). She had to select the picture that was related to the message and write its name. This task aimed to demonstrate how Rachel could use her written words to convey at least part of a message. We also repeatedly prompted Rachel to attempt writing when communication broke down.

After this therapy Rachel made further gains in her written picture naming. She also improved on a task in which she was asked to write a word in response to a given scenario ("What could you write if you wanted to watch the news?" target: TELEVISION). Most encouragingly, there were now instances in which Rachel used her writing in her daily interactions. For example, she wrote "HAIR" (a practised word) to indicate that a proposed therapy session clashed with her hairdresser appointment.

Therapy with Rachel did not resolve her severe aphasia. However, it significantly improved her written vocabulary and helped to overcome some of her communication difficulties. This study began 18 months after Rachel's stroke, so shows that therapy gains do not just happen in the early stages of rehabilitation. Perhaps most importantly, a follow up study showed that ten other people with Wernicke's aphasia benefited from similar treatment approaches (Robson et al., 2001)

a conversation between a researcher, Susie Parr, and Terry, who has severe aphasia:

> I ask what he will do today and he shrugs and then makes a pulling movement with his hands and points to the window. 'Over there'. I think for a minute. 'Fishing?' No. He makes a repetitive side to side movement with his hands and points out of the window: 'That'. The hedge is waving wildly and I say: 'Trim the hedge?' and he says 'That's it that's it'.. What will he have for lunch? He mimes a chicken by tucking his hands into his armpits, raising and lowering his elbows and clucking. 'Chicken?' 'That's it'.
>
> (Parr, 2007, p 123)

Despite using virtually no spoken words, Terry successfully conveys his plans for the day and his lunch menu. He uses a range of gesture types, including pointing, mime, and vocal gesture (clucking). He can also modify his gestures, when his first attempt is unclear.

Terry's skills with gesture are a bit unusual. Research has shown that many people with severe aphasia struggle to use gestures in their communication. They may gesture very rarely or produce non-specific gestures that are difficult to interpret. Such individuals may benefit from therapy focussing on gesture. This aims to facilitate gesture production and enable the person to exploit gestures, particularly when communication breaks down. In effect, we are hoping that the person ends up like Terry.

Gesture therapies often focus on a set of items, chosen for their practical relevance. A gesture for each item is agreed and practised. For example, "beer" may be gestured by miming pulling a pint or holding and drinking from an imaginary tankard. Each gesture is practised, usually in response to pictures. If necessary, the therapist will provide cues by modelling the gesture or even helping to shape the person's hands. Therapies may also incorporate communicative tasks. For example, the person with aphasia may be required to communicate the content of hidden pictures to their spouse using their practised gestures. Anna Caute and colleagues used these approaches with a group of people who had severe aphasia. The group learnt a set of gestures and improved on communication tasks, e.g., where they had to convey the content of a silent video to their partner (Caute et al., 2013).

Non-verbal strategies are not confined to gesture. Carol Sacchett and colleagues describe how a group of people with severe aphasia learnt to use drawing in their communication (Sacchett et al., 1999). Therapy targeted "generative drawing", that is the ability to call up an idea and translate that idea into a drawing. It also promoted "economic" drawing, i.e., drawings that home in on distinguishing features and omit unnecessary details. Participants were encouraged to think about the needs of the person interpreting the drawing and learnt to modify their drawings if they were unclear. Some time was also spent with communication partners (such as spouses) to improve their skills in interpreting drawings. Here are some examples of the therapy tasks that were used with one person in the study (GJ):

Aim: To focus on distinguishing features in drawings

Task: GJ had to add details to a base shape, in order to represent a named item; e.g., a square had to be modified to represent a washing machine and a circle modified to represent a clock.

Aim: To improve generative drawing

Tasks: GJ had to think of and draw all the things he might find in a shed. On another occasion he was asked to draw what he had for dinner the previous night.

Aim: To promote the use of drawing in conversation

Task: GJ was asked to describe his job using drawings.

At several points in therapy, GJ had to use drawing to convey messages to his wife. For example, he was given a target word which he had to get across in drawing. If his drawing was unclear, he was encouraged to enlarge parts, add details, or provide additional clues, e.g., in the form of a gesture. She was advised on strategies that she could use to interpret the drawing, such as asking "homing in questions" ("is it something in the garden?").

Figure 7.2 reproduces a drawing produced by GJ in therapy. It illustrates his former job as a tug boat skipper. In the second and third images he adds detail and uses enlargement to show how many barges he pulled and their contents.

Figure 7.2 Example of a drawing produced in therapy by GJ (Sacchett et al., 1999)

The participants in Sacchett et al. (1999) improved on an assessment of drawing following therapy. Comments from partners also suggested that some were using their drawing at home, and that it was having a positive impact on communication:

> *He wanted some painting done outside and he kept pointing with his walking stick and I didn't know what he meant, he just kept pointing to the brickwork you know … every time he went out he sort of looked at the side of the bungalow … and I said no what do you want? and he couldn't tell me but when we got indoors he drew the side of the bungalow and then was going like this* (makes a painting gesture).
>
> (quoted in Sacchett et al., 1999, p 278)

My final example of communication therapy is termed "Multi-Modality Aphasia Therapy" or M-MAT (Rose & Attard, 2011). This group therapy involves interactive communication tasks, for example in which participants have to request picture cards from each other. If they are unable to do this spontaneously, the therapist offers a series of cues, encouraging them to employ different communication techniques. So, the first cue invites them to gesture and name the target. If this is not possible, the therapist provides the gesture and word for the person to copy. The next cue invites the person to draw the item, again alongside the spoken word; and in the final cue the written word is provided for the person to read aloud and repeat. This therapy aims to improve speech through multi-modal cues. It also promotes strategies to use if speech fails; i.e., the person is encouraged to try gesturing or drawing if they cannot think of a word. A recent study showed that M-MAT was effective in improving measures of everyday communication, quality of life and the spoken naming of practised words. The treatment was compared to an alternative therapy that only focussed on speech production, and interestingly, results were similar (Rose et al., 2022).

WORKING WITH PARTNERS

Several of the therapies described so far involved communication partners. In most cases, this was to promote **generalisation** of skills to everyday communication. For example, in a typical format, the person with aphasia learns a strategy that is then practised in a task involving their spouse, so emphasising how that strategy might be used in their daily lives.

Involving partners can also develop their skills in using "aphasia friendly" communication techniques, such as avoiding complex sentences, accompanying speech with gestures, and giving the person time to get their message across. Therapy can help partners understand the specific features of their family member's aphasia, such as their comprehension levels or the nature of their speech errors. There is a further reason for working with partners. The last chapter described some of the negative impacts of aphasia on family members. Their needs for information and support should not be ignored in rehabilitation.

Support for partners can be delivered in a number of formats. Some therapists offer groups for family members. Here relatives can learn about aphasia and develop techniques to ease communication. Many also value the opportunity to meet others with an aphasic relative, to share their experiences and support one another.

Other therapy approaches are more individualised. Researchers at University College London have developed a therapy programme called "Better Conversations with Aphasia" (Beeke et al., 2013). Here, the aphasic person and their partner are videoed during conversations at home. The videos are analysed to explore patterns in the conversation and to pinpoint behaviours that either support or hinder its success. These behaviours are then targeted in therapy.

This programme was used with Barry and his wife Louise (Beeke et al., 2014). Barry had aphasia with word finding difficulties and agrammatism, i.e., his speech lacked sentence structure. Analysis of several home-based conversations showed that these often ran into trouble when Barry was stuck for a word. On some occasions he was able to write the blocked target. Louise's response on these occasions was interesting, in that she often asked Barry to say the word aloud. This ignored the fact that Barry had already got his message across and tended to further derail the conversation as Barry struggled to read what he had written.

Barry and Louise received eight sessions of therapy. In early sessions they viewed clips of their conversations and discussed what worked and what didn't work. This enabled them to identify behaviours that they wanted to change. For example, Barry decided to increase his use of writing and drawing while Louise opted to "let the conversation continue". They then practised their target behaviours in videoed role plays, which were, in turn, the focus of discussion and feedback. Recordings of conversations after therapy revealed some important changes. In line with their aims, Barry was using more writing and Louise was no longer insisting that Barry should read aloud what he had written. Her reflections on therapy showed that she had a new appreciation of how communication can be achieved in aphasia:

> *Well it made us realise that it doesn't matter how you converse. You don't have to talk, you can use tools such as writing, gestures, y'know and it doesn't matter, as long as you find your way of communicating* (quoted from Beeke et al., 2014, p 303)

ADDRESSING THE SOCIAL AND EMOTIONAL CONSEQUENCES OF APHASIA

In the last chapter we heard about the many negative impacts of aphasia on emotional wellbeing and quality of life, with risks of depression and social isolation being particularly high. A number of interventions aim to counter these risks.

A widespread approach here is the use of social support groups, such as those run by the UK Stroke Association and other charities. Often staffed by volunteers, these groups provide a venue for social contact and conversation. They are a place where people with aphasia can practise communication and feel understood; and are a safe setting where aphasic errors can be made without loss of face. Above all they provide an opportunity to meet other people with aphasia and to know that you are not alone.

Some groups for people with aphasia focus on cultural activities, such as drama, music or art (Pieri et al., 2023). As well as social contact, these offer outlets for creative expression. They can provide a space in which aphasia is forgotten, as the person becomes absorbed in producing a painting, or responding to music. Choirs for people with aphasia capitalise on the fact that singing familiar song lyrics is often possible in aphasia, even when speech is extremely limited. Choirs may also help to prevent depression, given the known effect of singing on mood.

Let me tell you about two inspiring examples of arts–based aphasia rehabilitation.

Cat Andrew has been running art groups for people with aphasia for many years, using her combined skills as a speech and language therapist and artist. In 2020 she linked up with the British Library and The Brain Charity in a project called "Seeing Sound". This used recordings from the Library's extensive sound archive as a stimulus for art. Cat and the Library sound archivist selected sounds relating to natural habitats, such as Coast and Woodland. For example, the coastal sounds included a recording from the Scarborough amusement arcade and the mating call of the haddock. Over five sessions, the 17 members of the art group listened to the sounds and responded by making works on paper using a variety of materials, such as charcoal, paint, and collage. You can see some beautiful examples in Figure 7.3. They shared what they had produced and discussed ideas and memories stimulated by the recordings. The groups engendered a wealth of artworks and had a profound impact on those involved. Here are some of Cat's reflections on the project:

> *Listening to sounds without language meant that language processing, which is difficult for people with aphasia, was bypassed. Instead, they could attune their ears and respond with their eyes and enjoy a full sensory creative experience without feeling frustrated by their language difficulties.*

> *The group members were incredibly creative, often unexpectedly to themselves. If you've got aphasia there is so much that is difficult,*

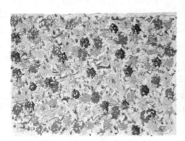 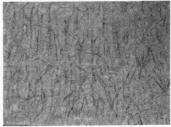

Figure 7.3 Art works produced by people with aphasia in the Seeing Sound project

effortful and inaccessible. Finding something in yourself that can be developed is so valuable. You can try out new things in a way that isn't pressured, but which is immersive and gives you a sense of progress.

My second example is Stroke Odysseys. Led by the charity Rosetta Life in collaboration with Kings College London and several NHS Trusts, this project creates performance art out of the personal stories of stroke survivors. Productions are formed in a series of workshops, in which stroke survivors work alongside professional singers, dancers, writers and musicians. The workshops take individual recollections and other personal narratives as stimuli for scenes in the performance, often involving a wonderful combination of speech, song, music, and movement. In 2018 Stroke Odysseys toured one of their productions round arts venues across the UK. As someone in the audience at a London staging, I can testify to the beauty and power of that production.[1] On the project website you can see videos of workshops and performances in progress (https://strokeodysseys.org). Those involved can also be seen talking about the impact of the project, for example on their confidence, communication, and sense of wellbeing.

Social and emotional therapies can involve stroke survivors in delivering the intervention. This acknowledges that people with aphasia are experts in their own condition and draws on that expertise. A good example is peer befriending. This is where someone who has had aphasia for some time is paired with a recent stroke survivor. In a series of visits, the peer befriender offers companionship and empathy, and shares their experiences of living with aphasia. They may also help the person to re-connect with community activities, for example by travelling with them on public transport. Benefits are potentially two-way. The befriendee can profit from the insights of someone who is an old hand at aphasia. They can learn that life with aphasia is possible, and gain hope. While the befriender is engaged in an interesting and valuable social role. A recent study explored the feasibility of peer befriending in aphasia and its impacts (Hilari et al., 2021). You can read about this study in Box 7.3.

Box 7.3   A Randomised Controlled Trial of Peer Befriending in Aphasia (Hilari et al., 2021; Northcott et al., 2022; Moss et al., 2022)

This study aimed to find out if peer befriending in aphasia is feasible and acceptable and whether it improves social and emotional outcomes.

Ten people were recruited as peer befrienders. They all had mild or moderate aphasia as the result of a stroke that happened at least a year ago. They demonstrated a number of personal qualities, such as good adjustment to their stroke, confidence, and a willingness to talk with others. Befrienders were given six hours of initial training and were provided with monthly supervision throughout the study.

Sixty-two other people with varying types and severities of aphasia were recruited to the study. They had fairly recent strokes (they were, on average, 40 days post stroke) but were discharged from hospital and had completed intensive rehabilitation. Following some early drop out, 56 of these individuals were randomly allocated to two groups. One group received peer befriending, while the other group did not, so acted as a control. Both groups continued to receive their "usual care". These were services that were already being provided. For example, they might consist of ongoing speech and language therapy sessions, or attendance at a social support group.

Those allocated to the peer befriending group were paired with a befriender. Wherever possible, pairings took account of common interests and other factors, such as age and gender. Each person received six visits from their befriender, followed by two optional follow up visits to help with the withdrawal of support. In the first meeting the pair agreed on goals and the schedule of visits. Subsequent meetings typically involved conversation, problem-solving discussions, and trips out. When asked about the content of sessions, befrienders described a wide range of activities including sharing stroke experiences, offering advice, talking about common interests, watching TV, playing games, knitting, going out to a café, and visiting a local stroke group. The agenda for visits was driven by the befriendees. This was nicely illustrated by Esther who befriended two individuals. In the first pairing she recalled talking about knitting and gardening, whereas in the second pairing conversation focused on geopolitical issues such as American aid to the Congo.

Participants in the study were asked to complete several questionnaires. These assessed their mood, feelings of wellbeing, their community involvement, feelings of confidence, and levels of social isolation. The questionnaires were administered three times by blinded assessors (i.e., the assessors did not know whether participants were in the peer befriending or control group). The first administration happened when the participant joined the study (baseline). The second was four months later, which for those in the peer befriending group was after their visits had ended. The final administration was ten months after the start of the study, so was a long-term follow up. All befrienders and a sub-set of befriendees were also interviewed, to capture their views about the intervention and any perceived benefits.

The feasibility results were good. For example, it was possible to recruit and train befrienders and support those befrienders during, in some cases, multiple pairings. The majority of participants completed their full quota of visits and very few people dropped out before the end of the study.

The interview transcripts showed that peer befriending was highly acceptable to both sides of the pairing. Those receiving visits often formed a strong rapport with their befriender and valued their experience as a stroke survivor. Some gained hope and confidence from their example. They described receiving advice, for example about local stroke groups or taxi card services, which they acted upon. Many recalled warmth and laughter during visits. Befrienders also spoke positively about the relationship with their pairs and found visits enjoyable and interesting. They felt that they were undertaking an important role and making a difference to the life of another person. For some, the experience resonated with their pre-stroke work life, so injected a feeling on normality. Although the role was demanding and occasionally stressful, all felt supported by the training and supervision.

Most of the questionnaire results showed only small differences between those who did and did not receive peer befriending. However, there was one striking finding. At the ten months assessment point 40% of those in the control group showed signs of serious distress on the mood questionnaire, compared to just 11% in the group that received peer befriending. Although only indicative, this may suggest that peer befriending helps a person to negotiate aphasia and fend off negative emotional consequences.

USING TECHNOLOGY IN REHABILITATION

Developments in digital technology offer fantastic opportunities for enhancing rehabilitation in aphasia. We now have apps for practising language tasks, devices that can circumvent aphasic problems and platforms for delivering therapy remotely. Let me give you some examples.

Language Practice Apps

We know that outcomes from aphasia therapy relate to dose, in that those who receive multiple sessions do better than those who receive just a few. Yet many speech and language therapy services struggle to provide the necessary amount of therapy, for example because of staffing limitations. This is where language practice apps can help. These are software devices that run on a standard home computer, tablet, or phone. They are designed for independent use by people with aphasia, so are easy to navigate. The apps typically provide a range of exercises, for practising different aspects of language. These exercises can be tailored, to manipulate levels of difficulty and to make them personally relevant to the user. Although designed for self-directed practice, data from the apps can be shared with a therapist. S/he can therefore monitor how the person is getting on, and potentially modify their exercises, to make them easier or more difficult.

Current widely used apps include TactusTherapy, StepByStep Aphasia Therapy, and Cuespeak. To illustrate further let's home in on Cuespeak (https://cuespeak.com). Designed for iPads and iPhones, this app offers 14 modules that work on words, sentences, and dialogues. Users can practise spoken or written language and target production or comprehension. Personally relevant material can be incorporated into the exercises, such as the names of family members, significant places, or pets. The app is also constantly updated, so includes material relating to current news events. Speech production is supported by videos of words and sentences being pronounced. Users can also record and play back their own speech. The exercises are presented in attractive, uncluttered frames, that make navigation highly intuitive, you can see an example in Figure 7.4.

There is a growing body of research showing that practice with computer apps can bring about significant improvements in aphasia. In one randomised controlled trial, 83 people with aphasia received six months of therapy using StepByStep aphasia software (Palmer et al., 2019). They carried out daily word finding exercises, targeting a

Figure 7.4 An example of a Cuespeak language comprehension exercise

vocabulary of 100 personally chosen words. Therapy was largely self-directed; i.e., each person worked independently at home on their computer. However, it was supported by monthly visits from a volunteer or therapy assistant. There were two control groups in the study. One was an attention control group (71 people). They did not undertake therapy but were asked to complete paper-based puzzles every day, such as sudoku and wordsearch. They also received supportive telephone calls from the research team each month. The second control group (86 people) undertook no additional activities and received no additional contact. Results showed that the computer therapy group improved on naming their 100 words. This improvement was still evident at a follow up assessment, six months after therapy had stopped, so was durable. The control groups were also tested on naming and showed minimal changes.

Circumventing Aphasic Problems

Many familiar, mainstream technologies have huge potential to improve the lives of people with aphasia by helping to compensate for their language difficulties. Examples are legion. Someone with little or no speech can take photos during a trip out, then use the pictures to tell the family about their day. A person with poor understanding of speech will struggle to use the phone, but may benefit from video conferencing technologies such as Facetime or Zoom where they can see the other person's face and gestures. Social media platforms, like WhatsApp, can be a means of retaining contact with friends and relatives, even when a person has minimal written language. Standard features of word processing software, such as spelling and grammar checkers, are also a godsend for those with impaired writing.

While some people with aphasia access these technologies independently, this is often not the case. Indeed, there are concerns that people with aphasia face digital exclusion, e.g., because language barriers make it difficult to download and use relevant software. This is where therapy can help. We can use speech and language therapy to train a person in using a relevant technology and enable them to exploit that technology to maximum effect.

A therapy project at City, University of London, helped people with aphasia to re-access reading and writing activities through technology (Marshall et al., 2018a; Caute et al., 2019). The writing arm used two technologies. One was a voice recognition software. Here, the user speaks into a microphone and the computer turns what they say into written text. This technology was selected by individuals who had better speech than writing. Those with more impaired speech used WriteOnline. This is a word processing software that incorporates several aids, including word prediction, vocabulary support in the form of individualised word bars, and text to speech conversion, enabling the user to listen back to what they have written. Each person received a two-hour introduction to their chosen technology followed by 12 hours of therapy. The latter refined their skills in using the technology and helped them to apply it towards individual writing goals. For example, some participants worked on emails, one wrote a story for their grandchild, and another produced a biographical account of their stroke. Therapy was augmented with homework tasks and supported by bespoke, easy-to-read manuals explaining each technology. This was a research project, so used a randomised controlled design. The primary outcome measure was an email writing task, scored for word count and grammatical integrity. Emails were also given a rating for how well they communicated their message. The 21 people who received therapy improved significantly on this task, and across all scores. The gain was evident only when they used their chosen technology to support writing. Unassisted handwriting did not change. The researchers, therefore, argued that therapy enabled the participants to compensate for their difficulties by using technology, it did not remediate those difficulties. Despite this limitation, the effect of applying technology was often transformative. For example, one participant could only write three words in his pre-therapy email ("the name ... the"). Whereas after therapy he wrote the following:

Dad,

Come on you Reds!

Good result. What did you think?

Team played really well. Liverpool 0 v 0 Southampton.

Wednesday 9/5/17

In the other arm of the City project, 21 people with aphasia learnt to use an assistive technology for reading. For example, many were assigned Kindle eReaders, which enabled them to adapt the formatting of text, look up word meanings in a dictionary, access plot summaries, and benefit from text-to-speech conversion. Participants received 12 hours of therapy in which they developed their skills in using the technology and addressed personal reading goals. After therapy, the group improved on a measure of reading comprehension and produced higher ratings for their reading confidence and enjoyment. Gains were only seen when reading was supported by technology, indicating that, as in the writing arm of the study, the effects of therapy were compensatory. Reports from those involved again pointed to the transformative effects of using technology. For example, one participant had not undertaken any reading since her stroke, other than attempts to use TV subtitles. Yet, after her eReader was introduced, she read news stories on the BBC app, two short books, and three full-length autobiographies.

Working Remotely

Many stroke survivors struggle to get to therapy. Physical disabilities make travelling to appointments hard, and domiciliary services may not be on offer. Of course, these problems are exacerbated if a person lives in a remote area. Here, tele-rehabilitation can help. This is where assessment and therapy are delivered remotely by using the phone or, more typically, video calls.

Researchers in Australia were among the first to attempt tele-rehabilitation in aphasia, partly driven by the need to reach a far-flung population. For example, they showed that it is possible to carry out aphasia assessment using video conferencing, and that those being assessed found the technology acceptable (e.g., Theodorus et al., 2008). A more recent Australian project showed that remote group therapy was possible, and improved outcomes on a quality-of-life measure (Pitt et al., 2018). At City, we ran a project in which ten people with aphasia received word finding therapy delivered remotely, using iPads and Facetime (Woolf et al., 2016). There were two comparator groups. One received the same word finding therapy but delivered face to face at the University. The other did not receive therapy but had conversations with students of speech and language therapy over Facetime. Our results showed that the word finding therapy improved naming of treated and, in some cases untreated words. Importantly outcomes did not differ between those who received remote and face to face therapy. The participants who were treated remotely were very happy with the format. They found the technology easy to use and enjoyed the sessions. Some were relieved that they did not have to travel. The participants who took part in remote conversation sessions did not improve in their word finding. However, they loved meeting with the students online and felt that the conversations were beneficial.

Using Virtual Reality

Video-conferencing is not the only way of working remotely. At City, we have developed a virtual reality platform that can host online aphasia therapy. We involved consultants with aphasia in the design. They advised us on the content and helped to determine how users would navigate and communicate within the platform. They emphasised that it should be fun and prioritised social interaction over formal language practice.

The end product of this co-design process was EVA Park (see figure 7.5). This is an online virtual island containing multiple locations, such as houses, a greenhouse, a café, a disco, a health centre, a hair salon, and a tropical bar. There are green spaces, in

(a)

(b)

Figure 7.5 A stroke survivor using EVA Park (a) and an appointment in the EVA Park hair salon (b)

which users encounter animals and birds, and a lake that is home to a giant turtle, a pearl oyster, and a mermaid. Users of EVA Park are represented by personalised avatars. These are controlled either from a regular computer keyboard or a simple keypad, and can walk, run, roller skate, or fly round the island. Users communicate with each other in real time via speech and, optionally, texting. There are interactive features that inject humour and fun. For example, the EVA Park disco contains a glitter ball, which when clicked makes your avatar dance.

What does EVA Park offer to aphasia therapy? As a multi-user platform it can host one-to-one or group meetings. It never closes, so users can meet up between scheduled sessions to chat or explore the island together. All EVA Park settings are colourful and fun. Users can enjoy the sun setting from a rooftop terrace, or float in an azure sea on a rubber ring. Deliberately bonkers, it is full of surprises and humour. Where else in aphasia therapy are sessions accompanied by a troop of penguins or a leaping dolphin? And people with aphasia can make their own jokes. Take Amy, a wheelchair user in her sixties, who opted to dress her avatar in a crop top, pedal pushers, roller skates, and a Mohican hair do; and take Jessica, who when invited to dive into the EVA Park lake declined because she had just washed her hair.

There are serious intentions here. EVA Park brings people together, so may help to counter the social isolation that often accompanies aphasia. The playfulness may increase motivation for therapy, encourage practice, and raise mood. For those with physical disabilities, being able to move freely round the island without the encumbrance of a hemiplegia is potentially liberating. When working on communication, EVA Park enables us to locate therapy in relevant settings. Cooking can be discussed in the EVA Park kitchen, and gardening in the EVA Park greenhouse. This lends authenticity to therapy and may help to extend therapy gains to everyday language.

We have run several research projects in EVA Park (e.g., Marshall et al., 2016, 2018b, 2020, 2023). These have shown that the platform can successfully host a variety of therapy approaches, including individual and group therapy, therapies targeting specific language skills, and social support. Results have shown improvements that are comparable to those achieved by face-to-face therapy. And, as illustrated by the quotes below, those involved in the projects were overwhelmingly positive about their experiences of using EVA Park:

> *Every day we went somewhere new, I love that.*

> *Tried them all. Sat on elephant. Swam on turtle. Dancing in Tardis and disco.*

> *I'm sitting right on the ... on a decking up the top ... of the houses ... and I'm thinking oh God I'm on holiday here.*

> *He's more confident in having conversations with people, whereas before he would hold back more. Now he's been more spontaneous. Talking about sports etc and I know he's been talking about the same topics in EVA Park. He's had a practice so he's extending what he's talking about outside. (family member)*

If you want to read more, Box 7.4 summarises our first EVA Park project.

Box 7.4   Using EVA Park to host communication therapy (Marshall et al., 2016; Amaya et al., 2018)

This study aimed to find out if EVA Park could be used to deliver an intensive programme of communication therapy and if users would find the platform acceptable. We evaluated the effects of therapy on measures of communication, confidence, and social isolation.

Twenty people with aphasia took part in the study. Each person received 25 hours of therapy delivered in EVA Park over five weeks. Therapy was led by support workers. Most of these were qualified speech and language therapists, although two were experienced stroke group volunteers. The support workers all received four hours training on how to lead therapy in EVA Park and were given weekly supervision.

Each participant was paired with a support worker and met with them daily in EVA Park. In the first session they agreed goals. For example, these might include asking questions, making requests or having more satisfying conversations. One participant wanted to prepare for giving a speech at his daughter's wedding. In the remaining sessions, the pair undertook a programme of activities addressing these goals. For example, one person practised requesting a hair cut in the EVA Park salon, with the support worker playing the role of the hair dresser, while another ordered food in the EVA Park restaurant. Asking questions was practised in conversations, for example about hobbies, TV programmes, and life events. Most sessions were one-to-one, but once a week participants and their support workers met in groups. This allowed for group discussions, for example about the news, music, and celebrities. One participant wanted to improve his ability to make points in an argument, so held a group meeting to discuss the merits of building a sports centre in EVA Park. The man who was preparing for his daughter's wedding gave a speech to his fellow participants in front of the EVA Park lake. We used an election narrative as a further stimulus for conversation. In this narrative four fictional candidates were standing for the position of EVA Park Mayor. Each candidate released a manifesto and was the subject of often scandalous news stories (one was exposed as a drug user, and another was caught having an affair). Participants expressed their views about the candidates' policies and discussed whether the scandals disqualified them for office.

The primary outcome measure for this study was an assessment of functional communication, in which the person had to answer questions relating to everyday scenarios, such as going to the doctor. Additional measures included questionnaires to explore feelings of confidence and social isolation. Participants completed the measures before and after therapy and six weeks later. They were also interviewed to capture their views about EVA Park and the programme of therapy.

We found that this programme of therapy worked well. Nobody dropped out and most people completed at least 88% of their scheduled therapy sessions. The participants expressed highly positive views about EVA Park in their interviews. They enjoyed the different settings and the varied activities on offer. Everyone felt a strong bond with their support worker, despite the fact that they had only met them in the virtual world and never face to face. Eighteen of the participants were able to identify positive changes in their communication as a result of their EVA Park therapy, such as talking more to family and friends. Twelve reported increases in confidence.

Results on the outcome measures were mixed. Scores on the assessment of functional communication improved significantly after therapy and this gain was still evident at the six weeks follow up. On the other hand, scores on the questionnaires were not affected by therapy.

This study showed that EVA Park can be used to target communication skills in aphasia and that it is very well received by its intended user group. Although not all outcome measures improved, comments from participants pointed to possible benefits that were missed by our measures.

SUMMARY AND REFLECTIONS

This chapter has described aphasia therapy approaches that aim to remediate language impairments, enhance communication, and improve quality of life. They use a range of techniques, such as language exercises, non-verbal strategies, and technological compensations. Delivery modes also vary, including one-to-one work with a therapist, group treatments and the involvement of communication partners.

In an ideal world, an individual with aphasia would have access to all these approaches, depending on their needs. Treatment should also be long term and address their changing priorities over time. So, early therapy might help the stroke survivor and family members to cope with the trauma of aphasia onset, and introduce strategies that maintain communication. Assessment will establish which language skills are most and least impaired and form the basis for setting treatment goals with the aphasic person. These goals might be addressed through specific language programmes and/or further work on compensation strategies. Useful technologies should be identified and practised. The person should have access to ongoing emotional and psychological support, for example through a support group or peer befriending scheme. And their family members should be similarly supported, perhaps through a relatives' group. As communication recovers, treatment goals should be re-calibrated, possibly to include uptake of new activities or even return to work.

By now, I can hear the hollow laugh of stroke survivors who have received nothing like this level of support. I can also sense the frustration of fellow therapists, who work in resource constrained contexts where this level of provision is a distant dream. Reconciling the often-yawning gap between our therapy aspirations and real life is a major challenge, and not one that is confined to the UK. I have met numerous therapists from Australia, North America, and other countries who express exactly the same frustrations.

What can we do to address this gap, beyond voting for a government that places a proper emphasis on public health provision? Several things can help. We have seen how the efforts of volunteers and charities can augment services, including volunteers who are themselves stroke survivors. We can try to be more cost effective, for example by using technology or delegating therapy administration to trained assistants. We can also experiment with different models of treatment delivery. Remote therapy moved from the exception to the norm during the 2020 COVID pandemic when face to face contact was proscribed. This continues to be used in many contexts, making therapy more widely available and reducing travel costs. In parts of Australia, North America, and the UK, therapists have been experimenting with a novel therapy format called Intensive, Comprehensive Aphasia Programmes (ICAPs; Monnelly et al., 2022). These programmes typically last for five or six weeks, during which the participants receive several hours of therapy each day, working both one-to-one and in groups. Individual goals are identified and addressed through language and communication exercises and by engaging with technology. For example, the individual may carry out self-directed exercises on their computer, or practice using software that compensates for their difficulties. Family members are also involved in ICAPs, for example by attending relatives' groups. Early research findings from ICAPs are promising (Monnelly et al., 2023). They show encouraging treatment gains, and positive views from those who have been involved. Of course, ICAPs will not suit everyone, particularly given the intensity of the workload, but I hope that they become one of the many forms of support on offer.

SUCCESSFUL REHABILITATION IN APHASIA

I began this chapter by saying that aphasia rarely resolves; and we have seen that in most treatment studies there are limits to what is achieved. This begs the question of what is a successful outcome in aphasia rehabilitation? In many ways this is an impossible question to answer, given the differences between people. However, let me tell you about one individual's story.

Sarah Scott had a stroke when she was 18. The circumstances were heart rending. She was reading aloud in class at school when she realised that she could no longer do so. The stroke was severe. In the early days, Sarah had minimal speech, and was unable to walk or swallow.

Sarah made an important and generous decision. She decided to make a video every year, usually around the date of her stroke anniversary and post these videos online. As it is now 14 years since Sarah's stroke, we have an invaluable record of her recovery and life with aphasia.

In Sarah's first video, nine months post stroke, her aphasia is still profound. Her speech is hesitant with word finding problems and limited sentence structure. She struggles to say her name and needs help with several phrases, such as "pins and needles". Although Sarah can write some words, she makes it clear that writing text is impossible, as is reading. Numbers are also a problem, for example Sarah is unable to say her age. It is clear that the stroke has had a huge effect of Sarah's life. Her plans to go to university are shelved and contact with friends is difficult. Although expressing a determination to "fight" she comes across as fragile.

Over the subsequent videos we see a transformation in Sarah. The change in her speech is dramatic. In her more recent videos she speaks in full, grammatical sentences. There are still word finding problems, but these are marked mainly by brief hesitancies before she manages to say the word she was looking for or sneaks in a cunning alternative. What is perhaps most impressive is the progression in Sarah's life. By five years post stroke she has a part time job as a science technician in a school. By year seven she has secured a full-time laboratory post with a major pharmaceutical company; and in more recent videos she refers to promotions. She is driving and alludes to an active social life with many friends. By video ten she is engaged, and in her most recent video she is married and living in her own house. Alongside her busy work and social life, Sarah is actively involved in awareness raising about stroke and aphasia, including an appearance on breakfast TV and presenting at the prestigious Royal Society in London.

For all these successes, Sarah is clear that her aphasia has not resolved. For example, in the lead up to her wedding she is anxious about saying the vows. Reading and writing are still difficult, and numbers remain a problem. Time and again she refers to the strategies that she uses to get round these difficulties, such as rehearsing important talks and using apps to assist with emails at work. She is living successfully with, not without aphasia.

What drove Sarah's recovery? She describes several episodes of therapy in her videos. At the start, she is receiving daily speech and language therapy. This is augmented by subsequent involvement in therapy research projects. Seven years after her stroke she attends an intensive therapy programme in America, following the ICAP model above, which she finds highly beneficial. In an early video she refers to an occupational therapy project which targets job-finding skills, such as CV writing. Her rehabilitation is also supported by a stroke group, which she helped to found. Of course, numerous personal factors are also at play. I admire Sarah's "can do" attitude and willingness, even eagerness to try new things; and a constant in all the videos is the obvious, unstinting support of Sarah's family.

Sarah's is just one story of how life can be rebuilt after aphasia. We cannot expect this to be replicated across all individuals. But we can hope for some key outcomes. I hope that people living with aphasia are able to recover effective and satisfying communication, even if the aphasia remains severe. I hope that they can retain, form, and enjoy personal relationships. I hope that they have access to new experiences and feel that there is progression in their life. I hope that their life feels meaningful and pleasurable. And, given that stuff happens, I hope that they have the support and personal strengths to cope whenever life gets really difficult.

NOTE

1 I found the Stroke Odysseys performance so moving that I cried. As I rarely indulge in public displays of emotion, I am only admitting this in a footnote.

REFERENCES

Amaya, A., Woolf, C., Devane, N., Galliers, J. R., Talbot, R., Wilson, S., & Marshall, J. (2018). Receiving aphasia intervention in a virtual environment: The participants' perspective. *Aphasiology*, *32*(5), 538–558. doi: 10.1080/02687038.2018.1431831

Beeke, S., Sirman, N., Beckley, F., Maxim, J., Edwards, S., Swinburn, K., & Best, W. (2013). Better conversations with aphasia: An e-learning resource. Available at: https://extend.ucl.ac.uk/

Beeke, S., Johnson, F., Beckley, F., Heilemann, C., Edwards, S., Maxim, J., & Best, W. (2014). Enabling better conversations between a man with aphasia and his conversation partner: Incorporating writing into turn taking. *Research on Language and Social Interaction*, *47*(3), 292–305. doi: 10.1080/08351813.2014.925667

Boyle, M. (2010). Semantic feature analysis treatment for aphasic word retrieval impairments: What's in a name? *Topics in Stroke Rehabilitation*, *17*(6), 411–422. 10.1310/tsr1706-41

Brady, M. C., Kelly, H., Godwin, J., Enderby, P., & Campbell, P. (2016). Speech and language therapy for aphasia following stroke. *Cochrane Database of Systematic Reviews*, *2016*(6), CD000425–CD000425. 10.1002/14651858. CD000425.pub4

Brady, M. C., Ali, M., VandenBerg, K., Williams, L. J., Williams, L. R., Abo, M., Becker, F., Bowen, A., Brandenburg, C., Breitenstein, C., Bruehl, S., Copland, D., Cranfill, T. B., di Pietro-Bachmann, M., Enderby, P., Fillingham, J., Galli, F. L., Gandolfi, M., Glize, B., ... The REhabilitation and recovery of peopLE with Aphasia after Stroke. (2021). Dosage, intensity, and frequency of language therapy for aphasia: A systematic review-based, individual participant data network meta-analysis. *Stroke*, *53*(3), 956–967.

Caute, A., Pring, T., Cocks, N., Cruice, M., Best, W. & Marshall, J. (2013). Enhancing communication through gesture and naming therapy. *Journal of Speech, Language and Hearing Research*, *56*(1), 337–351. doi: 10.1044/1092-4388(2012/11-0232)

Caute, A., Woolf, C., Wilson, S., Stokes, C., Monnelly, K., Cruice, M., Bacon, K., & Marshall, J. (2019). Technology-enhanced reading therapy for people with aphasia: Findings from a quasi-randomized waitlist controlled study. *Journal of Speech Language and Hearing Research*, *62*(12), 4382–4416. doi: 10.1044/2019_JSLHR-L-18-0484. PMID: 31765277

Cramer, S. C. (2008). Repairing the human brain after stroke: I. Mechanisms of spontaneous recovery. *Annals of Neurology*, *63*(3), 272–287. 10.1002/ana.21393

Efstratiadou, E. A., Papathanasiou, I., Holland, R., Varlokosta, S., & Hilari, K. (2019). Efficacy of Elaborated Semantic Features Analysis in aphasia: A quasi-randomised controlled trial. *Aphasiology*, *33*(12), 1482–1503. doi: 10.1080/02687038.2019.1571558

Hilari, K., Behn, N., James, K., Northcott, S., Marshall, J., Thomas, S., Simpson, A., Moss, B., Flood, C., McVicker, S., & Goldsmith, K. (2021). Supporting wellbeing through peer-befriending (SUPERB) for people with aphasia: A feasibility randomised controlled trial. *Clinical Rehabilitation*, *35*(8), 1151–1163. 10.1177/0269215521995671

Kiran, S., & Thompson, C. K. (2019). Neuroplasticity of language networks in aphasia: Advances, updates, and future challenges. *Frontiers in Neurology*, *10*, 295. doi: 10.3389/fneur.2019.00295

Kojima, T., Mimura, M., Auchi, K., Yoshino, F., & Kato, M. (2011). Long-term recovery from acquired childhood aphasia and changes of cerebral blood flow. *Journal of Neurolinguistics*, *24*(1), 96–112. 10.1016/j.jneuroling.2010.09.001

Marshall, J., Booth, T., Devane, N., Galliers, J., Greenwood, H., Hilari, K., Talbot, R., Wilson, S., & Woolf, C. (2016). Evaluating the benefits of aphasia intervention delivered in virtual reality: Results of a quasi-randomised study. *PloS One*, *11*(8), e0160381. 10.1371/journal.pone.0160381

Marshall, J., Caute, A., Chadd, K., Cruice, M., Monnelly, K., Wilson, S., & Woolf, C. (2018a). Technology enhanced writing therapy for people with aphasia: Results of a quasi-randomised waitlist controlled study. *International Journal of Language and Communication Disorders*, *54*(2), 203–220. doi: 10.1111/1460-6984.12391

Marshall, J., Devane, N., Edmonds, L., Talbot, R., Wilson, S., Woolf, C., & Zwart, N. (2018b). Delivering word retrieval therapies for people with aphasia in a virtual communication environment. *Aphasiology*, *32*(9), 1054–1074. doi: 10.1080/02687038.2018.1488237

Marshall, J., Devane, N., Talbot, R., Caute, A., Cruice, M., Hilari, K., et al. (2020) A randomised trial of social support group intervention for people with aphasia: A novel application of virtual reality. *PLoS One*, *15*(9), e0239715. 10.1371/journal.pone.0239715

Marshall, J., Devane, N., Berraondo, J., Talbot, R., Temponera, P., Clegg, K., & Wilson, S. (2023). Delivering script therapy for people with aphasia in EVA park: Two single case treatment studies. *Advances in Communication and Swallowing*, 1–12. Pre-press. doi:10.3233/acs-220014.

Monnelly, K., Marshall, J., & Cruice, M. (2022). Intensive comprehensive aphasia programmes: A systematic scoping review and analysis using the TIDieR checklist for reporting interventions. *Disability and Rehabilitation*, *44*(21), 6471–6496. 10.1080/09638288.2021.1964626

Monnelly, K., Marshall, J., Dipper, L., & Cruice, M. (2023). A systematic review of intensive Comprehensive Aphasia Programmes – who takes part, what is measured, what are the outcomes? *Disability and Rehabilitation*, 1–15. 10.1080/09638288.2023.2274877

Moss, B., Behn, N., Northcott, S., Monnelly, K., Marshall, J., Simpson, A., Thomas, S., McVicker, S., Goldsmith, K., Flood, C., & Hilari, K. (2022). "Loneliness can also kill": A qualitative exploration of outcomes and experiences of the SUPERB peer-befriending scheme for people with aphasia and their significant others. *Disability and Rehabilitation*, *44*(18), 5015–5024. 10.1080/09638288.2021.1922519

Northcott, S., Behn, N., Monnelly, K., Moss, B., Marshall, J., Thomas, S., Simpson, A., McVicker, S., Flood, C., Goldsmith, K., & Hilari, K. (2022). "For them and for me": A qualitative exploration of peer befrienders' experiences supporting people with aphasia in the SUPERB feasibility trial. *Disability and Rehabilitation*, *44*(18), 5025–5037. 10.1080/09638288. 2021.1922520

Palmer, R., Dimairo, M., Cooper, C., Enderby, P., Brady, M., Bowen, A., Latimer, N., Julious, S., Cross, E., Alshreef, A., Harrison, M., Bradley, E., Witts, H., & Chater, T. (2019). Self-managed, computerised speech and language therapy for patients with chronic aphasia post-stroke compared with usual care or attention control (big CACTUS): A multicentre, single-blinded, randomised controlled trial. *Lancet Neurology*, *18*(9), 821–833. 10.1016/S1474-4422(19)30192-9

Parr, S. (2007). Living with severe aphasia: Tracking social exclusion. *Aphasiology*, *21*(1), 98–123. 10.1080/02687030600798337

Pieri, M., Foote, H., Grealy, M., Lawrence, M., Lowit, A. & Pearl, G. (2023) Mind-body and creative arts therapies for people with aphasia: A mixed-method systematic review. *Aphasiology*, *37*(3), 504–562. doi: 10.1080/02687038.2022.2031862

Pitt, R., Theodoros, D., Hill, A., & Russell, T. (2018). The impact of the telerehabilitation group aphasia intervention and networking programme on communication, participation, and quality of life in people with aphasia. *International Journal of Speech-Language Pathology*, pmid:30200788

REhabilitation and recovery of peopLE with Aphasia after StrokE (Release). (2021). Predictors of poststroke aphasia recovery: A systematic review-informed individual participant data meta-analysis. *Stroke*, *52*(5), 1778–1787. 10.1161/STROKEAHA.120.031162

Robson, J., Pring, T., Marshall, J., Morrison, S., & Chiat, S. (1998). Written communication in undifferentiated jargon aphasia: A therapy study. *International Journal of Language and Communication Disorders*, *33*, 305–328.

Robson, J., Marshall, J., Chiat, S., & Pring, T. (2001). Enhancing communication in jargon aphasia: A small group study of writing therapy. *International Journal of Language and Communication Disorders*, *36*(4), 471–488.

Rose, M., & Attard, M. (2011). *Multi-Modality Aphasia Therapy (M-MAT): A Procedural Manual*. Melbourne: La Trobe University.

Rose, M. L., Nickels, L., Copland, D., Togher, L., Godecke, E., Meinzer, M., Rai, T., Cadilhac, D. A., Kim, J., Hurley, M., Foster, A., Carragher, M., Wilcox, C., Pierce, J. E., & Steel, G. (2022). Results of the COMPARE trial of constraint-induced or multimodality aphasia therapy compared with usual care in chronic post-stroke aphasia. *Journal of Neurology, Neurosurgery and Psychiatry*, *93*(6), 573–581. 10.1136/jnnp-2021-328422

Sacchett, C. Byng, S., Marshall, J., & Pound, C. (1999). Drawing together: Evaluation of a therapy programme for severe aphasia. *International Journal of Language & Communication Disorders*, *34*(3), 265–289. 10.1080/136828299247414

Saur, D., Lange, R., Baumgaertner, A., Schraknepper, V., Willmes, K., Rijntjes, M., & Weiller, C. (2006). Dynamics of language reorganization after stroke. *Brain*, *129*(6), 1371–1384. 10.1093/brain/awl090

Theodoros, D., Hill, A., Russell, T., et al. (2008). Assessing acquired language disorders in adults via the Internet. *Journal of Telemedicine and e-Health*, *14*, 552–559.

Woolf, C., Caute, A., Haigh, Z., Galliers, J. R., Wilson, S., Kessie, A., Hirani, S. P., Hegarty, B., & Marshall, J. (2016). A comparison of remote therapy, face to face therapy and an attention control intervention for people with aphasia: A quasi-randomised controlled feasibility study. *Clinical Rehabilitation*, *30*(4), 359–373. doi: 10.1177/0269215515582074

Worrall, L., Sherratt, S., Rogers, P., Howe, T., Hersh, D., Ferguson, A., & Davidson, B. (2011). What people with aphasia want: Their goals according to the ICF. *Aphasiology*, *25*(3), 309–322. doi: 10.1080/02687038.2010.508530

GLOSSARY

Agrammatism A lack of sentence structure. Agrammatic speech in aphasia has verb omissions and limited word order. Inflections, such as tense markers on verbs, are typically omitted and there are few closed class words. Agrammatism is a feature of Broca's aphasia.

Agraphia An impairment in writing, also referred to as dysgraphia. Acquired agraphia, e.g., following stroke, refers to the loss of previous writing skills. Agraphia is a common symptom of aphasia.

Alexia An impairment in reading, also referred to as dyslexia. Following stroke there may be an acquired alexia. This is where pre-stroke reading skills are lost. Alexia is a common symptom of aphasia.

Anomia A word finding problem. Anomia is marked by speech hesitancies, as the person searches for the words they want to use. There are often word errors, which may be semantically or phonologically related to the target. In severe cases very few words can be produced.

Anomic Aphasia A type of aphasia in which anomia (a word finding problem) is the main symptom.

Anosognosia A lack of awareness of a neurological deficit. For example, the person may deny having any paralysis despite being dependent on a wheelchair. People with Wernicke's aphasia often display anosognosia for their disordered speech.

Aphasia An acquired language impairment, affecting speech, reading, writing, and the comprehension of speech. It is usually caused by stroke but can follow other types of brain injury. It may also be referred to as dysphasia.

Apraxia A problem with the planning and execution of speech movements. If apraxia is severe speech may be impossible. Milder impairments result in unclear speech with pronunciation errors. The disorder may also be referred to as dyspraxia.

Arcuate fasciculus Neural fibres in the brain connecting Broca's area to Wernicke's area.

Bias In the context of research, bias refers to failings in the methodology that make one outcome more likely than another. When researching treatment effects there are many potential risks of bias. These include (but are not confined to) inadequate participant numbers for the design, the use of outcome measurements that have not been fully researched, and employing testers who are aware of whether or not the participants have received therapy (see 'Blinded Assessors').

Bilingual Being bilingual means you are able to use two (or more) languages. See Bilingualism.

Bilingualism The ability to use two (or more) languages. Patterns of bilingualism vary, depending on acquisition history and use. For example, one person may have a second language that was acquired at school, and which is less proficient than their L1; while another person, who was raised in a bilingual household, may have parallel competencies across both their languages.

Blinded Assessors Blinding of assessors aims to reduce bias in research. It means that the researchers administering tests with participants are not aware of key features of the research design. When researching treatment outcomes, blinded assessors do not know which participants have received therapy. This helps to ensure that they cannot, unwittingly, skew the data in favour of one outcome.

Brain Plasticity The ability of the brain to reorganise its structure and/or connections in response to novel events, such as brain damage.

Broca's Aphasia A non-fluent form of aphasia marked by hesitant speech with word finding difficulties and agrammatism (omissions in sentence structure). It is often accompanied by apraxia.

Broca's Area A region in the left frontal lobe of the brain that plays an important, although still not fully understood role in language. It is named after Paul Broca, a 19th-century scientist, who first identified the region. Damage to Broca's area is associated with Broca's aphasia.

Circumlocution A response to a word finding block in which the speaker describes features of the target, for example saying "you eat it" for apple.

Closed Class Words A fixed set of words that play a mainly grammatical role in the language, such as determiners (the), pronouns (he) and auxiliary verbs (he *was* walking). They are closed class in that new items are not being added to the set; e.g., we are not creating new determiners. Closed class words may also be referred to as function words.

Code Switching A bilingual phenomenon in which speakers import words and phrases from one language when speaking in another. For example, when conversing in English a bilingual speaker might introduce words from German. Code switching typically only occurs in conversations between bilinguals who share the same languages. In other words, a bilingual speaker will not code switch when speaking with a monolingual.

Cognates Words from different languages that have a common ancestor. Most cognates are therefore similar in form. An example is the term for night which is similar across English ("night"), French ("nuit"), and German ("nacht").

Cognitive Control The conscious exertion of control over speech or any other cognitive task. For example, we use cognitive control to edit expletives or other inappropriate uses of language when we are in a formal situation. Bilingual speakers have to exert cognitive control in order to stay within the target language e.g., to prevent them from slipping into L1 when speaking in L2. Their experience of controlling language selection may give them elevated skills in cognitive control.

Computerised Tomography (CT) An imaging technique that uses X-rays and computer processing to create detailed, cross-sectional, images of the body. It is one of the methods used to scan the brain.

Conduction Aphasia A type of aphasia featuring word finding difficulties, frequent phonological errors, and poor repetition of words.

Conduite d'approche A phenomenon seen in conduction aphasia in which there are strings of phonological errors related to a target word, such as "cable, taggle, tibble" for table. The string often gets closer to the target and may even end with the correct word.

Content Words The words that carry most of the meaning in a sentence, i.e., the nouns, main verbs, adjectives, and adverbs. Content words contrast with function words. The latter are words that play a mainly grammatical role, such as determiners (the), pronouns (he) and auxiliary verbs (he *was* walking). Content and function words are also referred to as open and closed class words, respectively.

Crossed Aphasia Rare cases of aphasia arising from a right hemisphere stroke in a right hander.

Declarative Memory Part of our long-term memory system that stores general knowledge and facts. It also has an episodic component that stores biographical recollections, or memories of personal events. Declarative memories are explicit, so are consciously recalled and can be easily described. They contrast, therefore, with implicit, procedural memories.

Deep Agraphia An acquired writing impairment in which both the whole word writing route and sound-to-letter conversion are impaired. As a result, very few real words or non-words can be written. There are multiple errors in writing, including semantic errors e.g., where "chair" is written as TABLE.

Deep Alexia An acquired reading impairment in which both the whole word reading mechanism and letter-to-sound conversion are impaired. As a result, few real or non-words can be read. People with deep alexia make multiple errors when reading words, including semantic errors, e.g., where CAT is read as "dog".

Differential Aphasia A phenomenon that can arise in bilingual aphasia where the impairments differ across languages. One language may be more impaired than the other, and/or the languages may display different aphasic symptoms.

Discourse A unit of language that is larger than a sentence, such as a narrative or conversation.

Dyslexia See Alexia.

Dyspraxia See Apraxia.

Ethnography A research method originally developed by anthropologists to study unfamiliar cultures. It involves observing and interacting with people in their own context and collecting multiple sources of data. These can include field notes of observations, interview transcripts, artefacts relevant to the area of enquiry (such as policy documents) and even the researcher's own reflections. Ethnographic methods have been used in aphasia research, for example to explore the practice of aphasia therapy and the experiences of people with aphasia.

Functional MRI An imaging technique that evaluates blood flow within the brain, so identifies which brain areas are active during a given task. Functional MRI scans are, therefore, conducted while a person carries out a given activity, such as reading words or thinking of the names of pictures.

Generalisation In the context of aphasia therapy, generalisation refers to the carry over of skills to novel stimuli or contexts. It is often difficult to achieve. For example, an aphasic client may demonstrate improved word finding when tested in the clinical setting, but with little carry over to conversational speech. For this reason, therapists often include tasks that promote generalisation, such as practising target words in role play or other communication activities.

Global Alexia A severe reading impairment in which even individual letters cannot be recognised.

Global Aphasia A severe form of aphasia in which all modalities (speech, reading, writing, and the comprehension of speech) are impaired.

Hemianopic Alexia An acquired reading impairment that is a consequence of a hemianopia, or the loss of vision in one visual field. It affects eye movements during reading, and particularly impairs the reading of text.

Hemiplegia A common stroke symptom in which there is a paralysis affecting one side of the body. The affected side is contralateral to the site of the stroke. So, if there is a paralysis following a left hemisphere stroke it will affect the right side of the body. Both the upper and lower limb (arm and leg) are affected by a hemiplegia.

Homophones Different words that share the same pronunciation, such as "bridge" (a structure spanning a river/a card game). As with "bridge" homophones may also be homographs or share the same spelling. However, many homophones have different spellings, such as "sole"/"soul".

Inflection   A modification to a word in order to express different grammatical features, such as tense (walk*s*/walk*ing*/walk*ed*) and number (house/house*s*). As in these examples, English inflections typically take the form of affixes to the ends of words.

Jargon   Fluent but incomprehensible speech, featuring in Wernicke's aphasia. Jargon usually contains neologisms, or non-word errors. When it is composed mainly from real words, it is referred to as semantic jargon.

Lesion   An area of damage within an organ or tissue, caused by an illness or injury.

Lexical Agraphia   See Surface Agraphia.

Magnetic Resonance Imaging   An imaging technique that uses magnetic fields and radio waves to create detailed internal images of the body. It is one of the methods used to scan the brain, for example following a stroke.

Morpheme   The smallest unit of meaning in a language. Unbound morphemes are words that are meaningful on their own, such as "kick". Bound morphemes only appear as additions to words, such as the inflection -ed in "kick*ed*".

Neglect   A neurological impairment in which one area of space (either to the left or the right of the individual) is not attended to. So, a person with left sided neglect may not notice objects or people on their left and may neglect the left side of their body in personal care. For example, a man with neglect may only shave one side of his face.

Neglect Alexia   An acquired reading impairment that is a consequence of neglect, causing the person to make errors with one side of written words. So, in left neglect alexia the person will miss-read the left side of words (i.e., word onsets in English). While in right neglect alexia errors are made on the right side of words (word endings in English).

Neologisms   In the context of aphasia, neologisms refer to non-word errors, such as calling a television "a talitus". Neologisms typically feature in Wernicke's aphasia.

Open Class Words   Categories of vocabulary that accept new members, e.g., to label new inventions. English open class words comprise nouns, main verbs, adjectives, and adverbs. Open class words contrast with closed class words, which are a fixed set. See also **Content Words**.

Paradoxical Recovery A feature in some cases of bilingual aphasia in which the person's second, or least used language recovers better than their first.

Peripheral Agraphia An acquired writing impairment that affects execution of writing. For example, knowledge of letter shapes may be lost, or the person may be unable to perform the hand movements needed for writing.

Phoneme A unit of sound in a word. Phonemes distinguish words; i.e., changing a phoneme will result in a different word ("hat"/"pat"/"mat").

Phonology The way that speech sounds are organised in a language. The phonological system determines which sounds feature in a language and how they combine.

Phonological Agraphia An acquired spelling impairment in which sound-to-letter conversion is impaired. As a result, spelling of non-words is particularly poor. The whole word spelling route is relatively intact, meaning that most real words can still be written. There may, however, be errors with closed class words (such as "the", "in", "but").

Phonological Alexia An acquired reading impairment in which letter-to-sound conversion is impaired. The problem is identified by poor reading of non-words. As the whole word reading route is relatively intact, most real words can still be read. People with phonological alexia may, however, struggle to read closed class words (such as "the", "in", "but"), and some display more general phonological problems. For example, they may make phonological errors in their speech.

Phonological Errors Speech errors that are related in sound to the target, e.g., calling a chair a "char".

Primary Outcome Measure This term is used in the context of therapy research. Studies that explore the benefits of therapy typically employ a range of outcome measures. In this case, the researchers should specify the primary outcome measure. This is the measure that is most predicted to change, because it is closely related to the content of therapy. See also **Secondary Outcome Measures**.

Primary Progressive Aphasia A form of aphasia that is not caused by a stroke. Rather there is progressive degeneration of the frontal and temporal regions of the brain involved in language processing. Symptoms vary according to which part of the brain is most affected and get worse over time. The condition is also referred to as Frontotemporal Dementia or Frontotemporal Lobar Degeneration (FTLD).

Procedural Memory The memory for well-rehearsed routines, such as riding a bicycle or playing the piano. The memory is implicit, so difficult to describe. For example, a person may remember how to ride a bicycle but would struggle to explain how they do so. The use of syntax in language is thought to be supported by procedural memory. In bilingual language use, the person's first language (L1) is thought to be more dependent on procedural memory than L2.

Prosody The rhythms and intonation of speech. Prosodic features help to convey the speaker's intentions, attitudes, and emotions. For example, excitement or irritation will be evident in a speaker's prosody.

Pure Alexia A condition in which reading is impaired but other language modalities are not. So, the person can still speak, write, and understand speech. Reading in pure alexia is slow and laborious, particularly with long words. It is often marked by letter-by-letter reading, in which the person names each letter in a word before identifying it.

Pure Word Deafness An unusual form of aphasia in which the understanding of speech is impaired, but other aspects of language are intact. It is caused by an inability to distinguish speech sounds. The problem is specific to speech, i.e., environmental sounds can still be differentiated and understood.

Randomised Controlled Design A research design that is used to assess treatment outcomes. In a randomised controlled trial (RCT) the research participants are randomly allocated to two or more groups. In a simple form of the design one group receives the treatment while the other, control group is given nothing, or a dummy treatment (placebo). Both groups are assessed over time on relevant outcome measures. Treatment benefits are demonstrated if the treated group improves on the measures significantly more than the control group.

Secondary Outcome Measures Studies that explore the possible benefits of therapy typically employ a range of outcome measures. These should be divided into primary and secondary measures. The primary outcome measure is most predicted to change because it is closely related to the content of therapy. Secondary outcome measures explore possible wider benefits from therapy. For example, a study of aphasia therapy may use a language test as the primary outcome measure. The researchers may hypothesise that improvements in language may have associated benefits for well-being, so include a quality-of-life questionnaire as a secondary measure.

Selective Aphasia   A phenomenon that can arise in cases of bilingual aphasia, where one language is impaired but the other is not.

Semantic Errors   Speech, writing, or sign language errors that are related in meaning to the target, e.g., where a horse is called "a dog".

Semantic Jargon   Jargon speech composed mainly from real but anomalous words. The meaning is obscured by multiple semantic and other types of errors. Semantic jargon is seen in some cases of Wernicke's aphasia.

Semantics   The meaning of a word, sign, or sentence.

Single Case Experimental Study   A research design in which there is just one participant. Single case studies can be used to assess outcomes from therapy. Experimental control is introduced, for example by assessing the person over time and showing that improvements only occur after therapy is introduced. Some aphasia studies also compare the person's performance on treated vs. untreated stimuli.

Surface Alexia   An acquired reading impairment in which the whole word reading route is impaired, making the person over dependent on letter-to-sound conversion. The disorder is identified by a regularity effect in reading; i.e., most regular words are read correctly but irregular words, like YACHT, are not. Non-words can still be read aloud, as these are handled by letter-to-sound conversion.

Surface Agraphia   An acquired writing impairment in which the whole word writing route is impaired. As a result, spelling is mainly accomplished by using sound-to-letter conversion. This causes errors with irregular words, such as "yacht" and "mortgage", which are not spelt as they are pronounced.

Sylvian Fissure   Also termed the lateral sulcus, this is a deep fissure in each hemisphere of the brain, separating the frontal and parietal lobes from the temporal lobe. The area around the Sylvian fissure is termed the perisylvian cortex. In the left hemisphere the perisylvian cortex includes Broca's and Wernicke's area and plays a key role in language processing.

Syntax   The way that words or manual signs are combined in a language to create sentences and express relational meanings.

Thrombolysis   The use of medication to break up blood clots. If used soon after a stroke it can restore blood flow to affected parts of the brain and improve outcomes. Not all stroke survivors are eligible for thrombolysis. For example, it is contra-indicated if the stroke is caused by a bleed rather than a clot.

Wernicke's Aphasia   A type of aphasia in which speech is fluent but difficult to understand, owing to the proliferation of errors. The speech is often referred to as jargon and frequently includes neologisms, or non-word errors. Awareness of the speech difficulty is typically poor, and understanding the speech of others is usually affected.

Wernicke's Area   A region in the left, temporal lobe of the brain involved in language processing, and particularly in the comprehension of language. It is named after Carl Wernicke, a 19th-century scientist who first identified the region. Damage to Wernicke's area is associated with Wernicke's aphasia.

Word Meaning Deafness   A problem with speech comprehension in which spoken words can be differentiated but not understood.

Working Memory   A short-term memory system that holds a limited amount of information for a constrained period of time. Working memory supports understanding of discourse, e.g., by retaining information that has already been stated.

INDEX

Locators in *italics* refer to figures.

Printed in the United States
by Baker & Taylor Publisher Services

Printed in the United States
by Baker & Taylor Publisher Services